SIS,

YOU ARE

HER

Healing. Evolving. Reclaiming.

YANIQUE P. WALTERS

COPYRIGHTED

Written by Yanique P. Walters
Cover design by Yanique P. Walters
Interior design by Yanique P. Walters
Edited by Blessing S. Ombugadu

Published by HER House Publishing
First Edition, 2025

Printed in the United States of America
www.yaniquepwalters.com

Sis, You Are HER!

This book belongs to:

_____

TO MY PAIN:

Thank you. You gave me a story.

And to every sister holding her own scars, may this book remind you that nothing you've walked through is wasted.

Prayers

God, thank You for using my pain as a vessel of purpose. Let these words reach the woman who needs them most. May she find healing, courage, and the reminder that she was never broken, only becoming. Help her to heal, evolve and reclaim everything that belongs to her.

Amen.

JOURNEY TO HEALING, EVOLVING & RECLAIMING

SIS, HERE'S THE JOURNEY

PART ONE – LET'S START WITH YOU

Chapter 1: Sis, The Mirror Doesn't Lie

Sometimes we don't even recognize the woman staring back at us. In this chapter, we go there, back to the names, the shame, the heartbreak, and the silence. But Sis, we also rise. You'll see what it means to reclaim your reflection, confront your broken pieces, and say out loud: "She's still in there." Because the mirror never lies.

Chapter 2: Sis, Are You Blocking Your Own Blessings?

Sometimes the love we ask for shows up, but we don't know how to receive it. We explore how fear, past trauma, and self-doubt can keep us from embracing the very thing we desire.

Chapter 3: Sis, You Are Not Alone

No matter how isolated you feel, there are women walking through the same fire as you are. This chapter is your reminder that your story matters and you don't have to heal in silence.

Chapter 4: Sis, Healing Is Messy, But Worth It

Healing doesn't look like a straight line. It looks like crying on a good day and laughing on a hard one. But the mess is part of the process, and it is worth every moment.

Chapter 5: Sis, Know Who's Sitting at Your Table

Not every smiling face is a safe space. We explore the importance of discernment in friendships and why emotional safety matters in your inner circle.

PART TWO – RECLAMATION & RESET

Chapter 6: Sis, Let's Talk Confidence
Confidence isn't loud; it's rooted. We break down the difference between self-confidence, self-worth, self-esteem, and self-value, and why you need all four.

Chapter 7: Sis, You're Not Difficult, You're Misunderstood
You weren't created to fit into every room, and shrinking yourself only buried your God-given gifts. This chapter explores what it really means to be misunderstood and why that doesn't make you hard to love or hard to handle.

Chapter 8: Sis, Let's Talk Boundaries
Boundaries aren't walls, they're doors. This chapter empowers you to stand up for your peace without apologizing. Boundaries help you choose yourself, protect your softness, and invite only what aligns with the woman you're becoming.

Chapter 9: Sis, You Are Not Hard to Love
You're not asking for too much, you're just asking the wrong person. We dismantle the belief that love has to hurt or be earned.

Chapter 10: Sis, Let's Talk Self-Love and Self-Care
Self-care is deeper than bubble baths and spa days. This chapter invites you to prioritize emotional, mental, and spiritual wellbeing. Because loving yourself out loud is the most powerful healing you'll ever do.

Chapter 11: Sis, Update Those Photos
It's time to release outdated images of yourself, literally and figuratively. You're evolving, and your environment and self-image should reflect that.

PART THREE – DISCERNMENT & DATING

Chapter 12: Sis, That's Not Love – That's Abuse

Abuse isn't always physical. This chapter identifies emotional, mental, and spiritual abuse, and helps you reclaim your power.

Chapter 13: Sis, That Man is Love- Bombing You!

The charm. The gifts. The over-the-top gestures. We expose the manipulative tactics of love-bombing and how to spot it before it sucks you in.

Chapter 14: Sis, He's Not Your Project

You are not his therapist, savior, or second mother. This chapter is a wake-up call for women who over-function in relationships.

Chapter 15: Sis, Trust Your Intuition

Your gut knows what your heart tries to deny. We explore how to recognize divine nudges and act on your inner knowing.

Chapter 16: Sis, Red Flags Aren't Decorations

Stop making excuses for what you clearly can see. This chapter helps you identify patterns, not potential.

Chapter 17: Sis, Someone's Been Playing Mind Games

Gaslighting makes you question your reality. We unpack how to spot it, how it shows up in relationships, and how to take your power back.

PART FOUR – REFLECTION & INSIGHT

Chapter 18: Sis, What Men Think But Don't Say Often

We hear directly from the men who took our survey. Their honesty, confusion, and confessions bring a new perspective to the gender divide.

Chapter 19: Sis, Know When He Is Being Intentional

Effort isn't confusing. When a man wants you, he shows it. We break down signs of genuine pursuit versus performative interest.

Chapter 20: Sis, What Makes A Man Choose 'HER'

We flip the script and ask the men how they recognized their partner. Their answers? Enlightening, surprising, and sometimes, sobering.

PART FIVE – BECOMING HER

Chapter 21: Sis, Single-Life is not Punishment

Being single is not a punishment, it's an opportunity. This season gives you space to discover who you are, grow in confidence, and build the kind of life that excites you. Think of it as your time to flourish, to invest in yourself, and to shine so brightly that the right people and opportunities are naturally drawn to you.

Chapter 22: Sis, Be True to Who You Are

Everything starts with truth, your truth. No one knows you better than you know yourself. People may misjudge you, misunderstand you, or even lie to you, but you owe it to yourself never to live a lie. This chapter is about owning your truth unapologetically and building a life that aligns with who you truly are, without faking it.

Chapter 23: Sis, Gratitude is a Must

We explore the healing power of gratitude even during painful seasons. Gratitude is not denial, it's alignment.

Chapter 24: Sis, Who Are You Without the Pain?

When your identity isn't tied to trauma, who do you become? This chapter is your permission to discover the healed version of you.

Chapter 25: Sis, Take Accountability

Blame doesn't solve problems, it only makes them heavier. True growth begins when you take responsibility for yourself and for how you show up in your relationships. This chapter explores what accountability looks like and why it matters.

Chapter 25: Sis, Attract What You Deserve

You don't get what you want, you get what you believe you deserve. It's time to raise your vibration and align with abundance.

PART SIX – RISING INTO HER

Chapter 27: Sis, You Are Still HER

Even when you feel broken, confused, or in between seasons—you are still powerful. You are still worthy. You are still HER.

Chapter 28: Sis, Let Go to Grow

This chapter explores how letting go of what no longer serves you creates space for growth. To get more, you must create space for it. That means releasing the old things that have been holding you down.

Chapter 29: Sis, Let's Conquer the World (Together)

This journey was never meant to be walked alone. We remind you that sisterhood, purpose, and joy are the true revolution.

REFLECTION

Chapter 30: Sis, Look How Far You've Come

A final love letter to your journey. You started this book seeking answers. Now, you leave it armed with truth, confidence, and a mirror that reflects your strength.

Chapter 31: Sis, Pass the Torch

You've done the work. Now be the light. And pass it on. This chapter invites you to share your healing, wisdom, and voice with the next woman who needs it.

PREFACE: SIS, FIX YOUR CROWN!

*"She is clothed with strength and dignity, and she laughs without fear of the future." – **Proverbs 31:25 (NLT)***

Hey Sis,

Thank you for being here. Let's talk for a second.

There are stories in this book, and while some are a reflection of myself, I have a feeling you might just see yourself in them too.

This book is about building back your confidence and reminding you of who you really are. Your confidence may be lacking right now, but we *got this!*

The truth is, I didn't come into this world doubting myself. And neither did you. God wasn't just going to send us out here already missing out, nah! He loves us too much to set us back like that. But somewhere along the line, maybe after that first heartbreak, maybe when life just kept swinging, we started shrinking. Not on purpose, but piece by piece, it chipped away. And just like that, our confidence eroded; slowly and quietly. Like a thief in the night, you never even saw it coming.

And sometimes, the way it sneaked up on us, we didn't even get the chance to name what was happening. We just knew something in us felt off.

For me, I had to go digging. I had to trace it all the way back. And that's when things began to shift. Now I'm here, holding up a mirror, hoping you'll again see yourself too. I want you to hear me when I say, it's okay if you feel like your crown has slipped. Heck, mine slipped too. Love had me confused. Pain had me lost. And fear? She had me silenced for *way* too long. I poured into people who barely noticed I was running on empty, just to please them. And for a while, I forgot who I was - my very essence, that which makes me stand out in the crowd - my identity!

But Sis… Here is the best part, I remembered. Hmmm, yeah. I picked that crown up, gave it a little wipe, tilted it just how it should be - like the queen that I am - heiress, then walked out with my head high like I never dropped it. Because that's the energy!

This book is partly a story, partly a soul-talk, and partly a "girl, me too!" conversation. It's filled with journal prompts, affirmations, real-life lessons, and truths I had to learn through tears.

It's for the women who gave too much for too little. For the strong friends holding it together through silent breakdowns. For the soft ones who loved loud but ended up healing in silence, without anyone knowing they were even hurt. It's for the ones who scroll through posts thinking, *"Whew… that's me."*

I know this isn't just my healing, because I had women fill a survey for this book. This is about *us*. I am sharing mine, hoping you will realize that needing help, staying in situations for too long, or questioning your worth doesn't make you weak. It makes you human.

This book isn't about perfection, it's about permission; to feel, to heal, to rebuild, and most importantly, to choose *you!*

If your crown is tilted or embracing dust, don't worry. We're not gonna judge it. We're fixing it. One chapter at a time.

Let's get right into it…

INTRODUCTION: SHE IS STILL IN THERE

"She is clothed with strength and dignity, and she laughs without fear of the future."
— Proverbs 31:25 (NLT)

Now that the crown is back on your head, let's talk about what's

underneath it because fixing the outside is one thing, but for real healing? That's an inside job.

Once you've dusted yourself off and stand tall again, then the real work begins - the inner work. The reflection. The re-learning. The becoming.

It starts with our mind, but our minds can be our greatest gift or our biggest enemy.

The fictitious stories we tell ourselves:

"I'm not enough".

"It's my fault".

"Maybe this is the best I'll ever get".

This can ruin what was meant to be beautiful. But at the same time, we can't ignore our intuition because that inner voice is our superpower. It's been there the whole time, whispering truth even when you chose to silence it, to sugar-coat it, or not to even believe it at all. Don't ignore it anymore. It's here to protect you, not punish you.

Sis, I don't want you thinking that I'm writing from the mountaintop. I am definitely not. I'm writing from the middle, the messy middle.

I'm writing from therapy sessions that cracked me wide open.

SIS, YOU ARE HER

From sleepless nights where I cried, prayed, questioned, and wrestled with old wounds that were still bleeding.

From moments I knew better... but couldn't do better. Heck, maybe I said I'm gonna do it anyways.

Sis, what I am saying is that I'm not perfect. I've missed the mark countless times. I've chosen potential over peace. I've confused struggle with loyalty. I've ignored red flags and convinced myself the vibes were just off. I've been hurt and at times been the one doing the damages. But then, I've also grown. I've been doing the work. And every day, I keep becoming - the version of me that my younger self would be proud of.

Every day I aim to be more like Jesus, but I know that only Jesus himself is perfect! But there is no harm in trying.

Sometimes in my quest to be better, I find myself downplaying my worth in an effort to not come off as too confident. I don't want people to feel small because of my presence. But I soon realized that doing that does more harm than good- I need not to play small just to make others feel better, when there's so much space in the universe for everyone to be as "big" as they can be; becoming all that's encoded in God's blueprint for their lives.

I think my perspective changed at a conference I attended. I got the opportunity to ask Stephanie Chung, a sought-after keynote speaker and author, a question that had been heavy on my heart. I said, *"When I downplay myself, is that humility... or am I just putting myself down?"* And her response stopped me in my tracks. She said:

> *"A person who does that is seeking validation. They probably already know they're capable, but they're waiting on someone else to affirm it. They don't want to be the one shouting it from the mountain top because they are afraid of how others would view them"*

Yup. I needed to hear that, but that was the moment the mirror was in my face looking at me and saying, *'girl I've been trying to tell you to stop that crap!'*

Can you believe that what I was doing was waiting for someone else to tell me I was good enough, smart enough, and lovable enough and loving enough. It was at that moment, that I made a vow to stop waiting for permission to be who I already knew I was.

Sis, that's what I want for you, too.

It's okay if you've been craving validation. We've all craved it at one point in time. We've all chased love in places that couldn't hold us- jobs, family, men, and friendships. We just wanted someone to stamp us as worthy.

I'm telling you, **YOU DON' T NEED THAT.**

You don't have to stay in relationships that leave you emotionally bankrupt. You don't have to keep toxic friends just because you've known them since childhood. You don't have to keep showing up in rooms where you're only tolerated and not celebrated.

It's time to slow down. To listen inward. To choose better. To treat *you* better.

I've been wanting to write this book for years. But fear kept whispering, *"Who are you to tell your story?"* And God kept resounding, *"Who are you not to?"*

If you're tired of shrinking... Then this is your mirror.

If you've ever whispered, *"Am I enough?"* — Then this is your answer. Read it. Highlight it. Cry with it. Share it. Let it work through you.

SIS, YOU ARE HER

By the time you close this book, I hope you're walking differently. Talking differently. Loving differently. I hope you meet yourself again, and this time, you don't abandon her.

So, Sis, straighten your posture. Wipe your tears. Look in the mirror and say this with me: She is still in there and the mirror will confirm it in the next chapter.

HER Mirror Moment: Sis, Say It Out Loud

"I am worthy of love, peace, and healing, right now, not later. What I'm facing will not break me. God's hand is still on me, and His plan is greater than my pain. I will keep going. I've got this… and God's got me."

HER Assignment: Write to Your Younger Self.

Before you flip to the next page, pause. This is sacred. Write a letter to the younger you, the girl who didn't know her power yet. The girl who tried to fit in. The one who gave so much of herself just to feel loved. The one who needed someone to say, "I see you, and I'm proud of you."

- Tell her what you now know.
- Tell her she didn't fail.
- Tell her she didn't deserve the pain.
- Tell her she has always been worthy.

And then thank her.

Because she survived… so **YOU** could become **HER**.

PART ONE

Sis, Face The Mirror

Unpacking the Pain, Finding the Woman Within

1

SIS, THE MIRROR DOESN'T LIE

"You can't fix what you won't face. Start by looking her - you, in the eye."
– Yanique P. Walters

I remember standing in the mirror, just staring, wondering, *who the heck is this woman?* When did I lose myself? And how do I get HER - my lost self-back?

Well… who *was* I? Let's talk about this.

I was born and raised in the beautiful island of Jamaica. Nuh whe no better than yaad! (Translation: "There's no place better than home."). Most people knew me as "Jenniemae big forehead, nanny buck-buck, dry-head, dutty (dirty) foot daughter." Yep, I had all the descriptions in the world. I wasn't shy of name-calling. If there's one thing about

Jamaicans, it's that they're going to let you know exactly how they feel about you.

And whew… that mess hit my confidence from an early age. I got teased for how I looked, and I shrunk into myself. The boys weren't checking for me, and there were never any solid relationships around me to model what love was supposed to look like. Sis, I felt lost… invisible.

So, I buried myself in books. I went to school and remained focused. Helped my mom in her businesses and took care of my younger siblings. That's really what my childhood looked like, but that's what comes with being the oldest child, right?

As I got older, I no longer wanted to be defined by name-calling anymore, it was time to shift my mindset.

I decided to own my look. I stopped trying to be what everyone else wanted me to be and started focusing on who I was. I built a relationship with God, and through that, I learned that I was created in His image. I may not have looked the way others wanted, but I definitely looked exactly the way God intended.

I still remember the day the shift really happened. I was walking through the streets of Spanish Town when a bus passed by. The conductor stuck his head out and shouted, "Forehead!!!" in a derogatory way and the whole bus erupted in laughter.

But this time? I shouted back, "Get used to it cause it ain't going nowhere!"

In my head I was screaming: *Give me back my damn power. Now!* Because that's exactly how I felt.

Afterall, this is the first thing people get to see whenever they look at me. So why should I let that bother me. Why should I remain stuck over what I obviously don't have the power to change?

So how do you show out when the world underestimates you? You go where you're seen.

I joined a modeling agency. Ripped the runway. I was on TV, doing fashion shows. I even landed on a center spread in the newspaper. I don't even know when I became *that* girl, but when I did, my confidence started to soar! My clap-backs were elite. My vibe was loud. People were checking for me, heck... men, started checking for me. *Stand in queue dude!* I eventually started feeling like I looked better than most of the people who made fun of me back in high school. Well, that was the confidence in me, talking! I just felt unstoppable. I was most definitely in my siren energy.

I was living in Vida Loca. Life was good! But then, I got pregnant with my amazing son, Kyng.

What should have been the happiest time of my life... wasn't.

I had moved all the way across the country, from Jamaica to the U.S., all because of love. Or so I thought. I was 30 years old and had this vision etched in my heart: married at 30, building a home, starting a family with someone who saw me, chose me, and loved me.

So, when he asked, I saw it as God's way of positioning me for my answered prayers.

And honestly, I still see it that way.

Because even though the relationship didn't last, I'm in a way better position now than I ever imagined. And truth be told, I wouldn't have had these experiences to share with you if it weren't for that journey. Moreover, I have always wanted to be a mom, so I was happy to have my son.

So, no regrets, God doesn't make mistakes.

But you may wonder, what do I mean by it wasn't the happiest time of my life. Well... Back in Jamaica, I was thriving. I had a great job. I was traveling the world. I started a business aimed at helping Jamaicans find online jobs. Been interviewed. Bought my own home. I was doing so much for myself.

But even with all of that, I still craved love, affection and a family. So of course, I said yes.

But after I got married and moved to America to be with my ex, the same man who once said he loved me started taking jabs at my confidence. Yup, we were right back where the pain started.

"You think you're all that because you have a master's degree... but wait until you take off the hair and the makeup", he would say.

And it hurts. I felt low again.

But the worst part? He left me, a month into my pregnancy. In a country where I knew no one. No family. No support.

I remember thinking... *I must not be worthy. Who does this to someone they love? Am I that bad? Am I hard to love? Does he not see value in me?*

I had a lot of questions for myself.

There was a night I was driving home alone, and as the sky darkened, a question kept echoing in my mind: *"Why did he marry me?"*, *"Why did he bring me to the US just to abandon me?"*

With every answer I tried to give myself, another scar whispered back: *You're not enough. You failed. You'll never measure up.*

Sis… that kind of doubt doesn't just bruise you. It *buries* you.

I felt defeated. I started questioning everything. My worth, my voice, my ability to love and be loved. I became snappy. Suspicious. I started self-sabotaging because letting someone get close again felt like inviting heartbreak to dinner. Like how can I truly do it again?

That's when I started seeking validation from men. I wasn't looking for love, I was looking to feel something. I craved attention, even if it was temporary. I fell for emotionally unavailable men because the little they gave me felt like a lot.

And the worst part? I was starving for affection and didn't even realize it. And while I wasn't sleeping with these men, just knowing they were there giving me attention, it felt enough.

Some of the men I attracted reflected where I was emotionally. I wasn't whole. I wasn't healed. I kept trying to build connections out of broken pieces, when I clearly do not have the glue it takes to keep it firm. I kept thinking, *maybe if I do more, give more, love harder… they'll care, they'll reciprocate. But nah, that didn't work, I guess they could see the lostness in my eyes.*

I would make excuses for them. I convinced myself: *He's just busy. I'm expecting too much. He will come around soon, just relax.*

SIS, YOU ARE HER

Sis, if you have ever told yourself any of these, when a person is not prioritizing you, I want you to know that when a man wants to show up, *he will*. And when he doesn't, that silence? That's your answer.

One night, sitting in my parked car, yup, that same car again (I swear that's where most of my revelations happen), I finally said it out loud:

"I don't want to do this anymore."

That night, I wasn't crying over anyone who's chosen to leave. I was crying for myself. For the girl I left behind, trying to be what someone else needed. For the woman inside me still waiting to be seen, by *me*.

And when I finally got up, walked inside the house, and stood in front of that mirror, something shifted. And I said it again, soft but certain: *I don't want to do this anymore!*

And for the first time in a long time, I didn't pick myself apart. I didn't see flaws. I saw a girl who was finally reclaiming her worth.

I just stood there... staring.

Then I whispered to my reflection:
"You're still in there, girl. I got you."

Right on cue, my son walked in and said,
"Mommy, you look good."

Y'all... I shed a tear.
That boy knows how to hit me right in the feels.
He sees me, sometimes in ways I forget to see myself.

That moment brought *her* back - the woman I buried. The one who once stood boldly, laughed loudly, and walked purposefully.

Sis, I am telling you this story because I don't want you to make the same mistake. It's easier to try to find distraction to bury the pain but it's better for you to take time to heal and reflect. You have so much inside you, so many gifts, so many stories, so much love the world is waiting for. Don't be that girl. Doing that doesn't wash away the pain, it only covers it up.

So, if you've ever looked in the mirror and struggled to recognize who you've become?

Sis… you're not alone.
But the woman you've been searching for?

She's still in there.

Let's go find her. And when you begin to discover her and step into everything your heart desires, sis, please don't block your blessings. Let's talk more about that in the next chapter.

HER Mirror Moment: Sis, Say It Out Loud

"I am not who they said I was.
I am who I decide to become.
I see myself clearly now, and Sis...
she's still in there—worthy, whole, and ready to rise."

HER Word: Sis, Let's Reflect

Now it's time to reflect, so grab your "Her Reflection" Journal and let's reflect on this chapter. Find a quiet spot. Light a candle if you're fancy or lock yourself in the bathroom if that's the only serenity you get. Now breathe. These questions aren't here to drag you; they're here to *free* you.

Write like nobody's watching. Be real, be raw, and be a little messy if you must. Cry if you want to. Let's get into it:

Your Reflection Questions

1. When was the last time you looked in the mirror and felt disconnected from the woman looking back at you?
2. What relationships or experiences made you question your worth?
3. What would it look like to celebrate yourself instead of waiting for someone else to do it?
4. What mindset shift would it take for you to put down your running shoes?

2

SIS, ARE YOU BLOCKING YOUR OWN BLESSINGS?

"You asked for more, but are you ready to receive it? Or are you pushing it away before it gets too close?"
– Yanique P. Walters

S is, I know I touched on self-sabotage earlier, but maybe you're still wondering what it really is. Let's break it down together.

Self-sabotage is when you finally start seeing the good things you've prayed for, the love, peace, consistency, and instead of embracing it, you find a way to run from it. It's that little voice in your head that whispers, *"This is too good to be true,"* or *"Girl, don't get your hopes high."* It's not just about fear, it's about protection. Your mind is trying to keep you from getting hurt again, but in doing so, it blocks the very good thing you deserve.

Now, if we're going by textbook, self-sabotage is the act of intentionally or unintentionally undermining your own success or happiness through behaviors that interfere with your goals and growth.

For me? It showed up in some real messy ways after my divorce.
If someone liked me too much, I assumed they were fake. If they were too available, I got bored. If they were consistent, I questioned their intentions.

I didn't know how to receive goodness.

Over the last few years, therapy revealed something wild to me. I was running from the very love I claimed I wanted.

Real talk? I was that girl in the Mooski song: *"She's a runner, she's a track star..."* If it felt too real, too healthy, and too good, I dipped.

I'd find reasons to pull back. I'd nitpick. I'd start preparing for the worst before anything even went wrong. Because in my mind, it was easier to walk away early than to be blindsided and broken later.

One of my biggest fears was being taken advantage of, so instead of waiting for the hurt, I left first, especially when my emotional needs were being met. It was like, *"Okay, thanks for the attention. Now I'll disappear before things get too real."*

I told myself I was being smart. I was protecting myself.

Why? Because deep down, I didn't believe I deserved it. Afterall, my ex-husband made me feel that way. I told myself maybe my family was cursed, because why was it so hard?

On one side there were broken patterns, and on the other, marriages that lasted. But I wasn't close to the latter side, to role-model their behaviors. So I was looking for external factors to blame for everything that was happening. Until I read '*The Mountain Is You*', by Brianna Wiest and whew, **light-bulb moment!** Sis… I was the mountain. I was standing in my own way, blocking my own blessings. No one else was to be blamed,

Self-sabotage for me wasn't about not feeling. It was about **not feeling safe enough to feel**. It wasn't that I didn't care, it was that I didn't trust anyone else to care for me when I was hurting.

I made strength my identity.
I treated emotions like problems to be solved.

Pain? Processed and packed away.
Sadness? Handled, quickly.
I didn't linger. I didn't pause. I didn't sit with the ache.

I rarely cried when things ended—unless I was really mad at myself for ignoring the signs and holding on longer than I should have. It wasn't that I wasn't sad, or torn, or questioning where I went wrong. I just learned early that I had to keep it moving. That was my survival mode. My way of staying strong when everything else felt shaky. And I had a little boy who needed me to keep going, no matter what.

But one day, a friend said something that hit me straight in the chest. "You're so heartless," she said.
Then she softened a bit. "It's like you shut your heart off when things end."

But even with the softened version, it still stung.

So I fired back quickly, "Why should I cry? If the relationship was already fading, what am I really losing? I've spent months grieving silently while trying to make it work. By the time it's over, my tears are already gone—dried up."

She looked at me and said, "Yeah... but that's the problem. You don't even let yourself sit in the feeling."

Whew. That was a moment.
A mirror I didn't even know I needed.
And the truth? She was right.

Let me clear something up: **I *do* feel.**
I'm not heartless—she doesn't believe that either, or she wouldn't be my friend. But compared to her (who will cry for days over a breakup), I just handled things differently.

Why? Because I've had to. And honestly, I cried so much as a kid that sometimes I wonder if I just ran out of tears. Just kidding... but not really.

And I know not everyone has the strength to walk away, and I'm not saying you should ignore your emotions or rush through pain. But you do have to know when enough is enough, so you don't lose yourself in the process. This will help when its time to rebuild. You don't want it taking too much work that you lose yourself in the process.

If you're trying, try your best.
But don't try to the point where you sacrifice your health, your peace, or your well-being.

As for me, I had to build the strength to survive things that were meant to break me. I've seen so much. I lived in survival mode for too long that I got used to skipping the emotions, pushing through, and moving on.

But in that process, I forgot how to pause.
To grieve.
To celebrate.
To reflect.

I had to relearn that:
It's okay to cry.
It's okay to feel joy.
It's okay to be proud.

I remember being the kind of woman who rarely showed her excitement, even when deep down I was overwhelmed with joy. I wasn't expressive. Not because I didn't want to, but I didn't know how to be. But I want you to know that showing emotion isn't weakness—it's being human.

And honestly? It's the pain that makes us invincible.
Because we felt it, showed it, yet we kept going.

So now, I let myself feel.
I show my excitement, my sadness, my anger.
Because it's okay to express what you feel in the moment instead of suppressing it and pretending it doesn't exist.

It's okay to cry and let it out.
It's okay to pause.
It's okay to be soft.

SIS, YOU ARE HER

Being strong all the time is not a superpower.
Being honest about how you feel—that's where the real power is.

Sis, it was so bad that I used to think vulnerability was weakness. But now I know, it's the exact opposite.

Vulnerability is powerful. It's the kind of strength that can't be faked. A person who can still be open, soft, and real, even after being hurt, that's real power.

Vulnerability can heal relationships. It can heal *you*.

So, let me ask you, Sis: Are you letting yourself be vulnerable?
Or are you lacing up those emotional track shoes and sprinting at the first sign of discomfort?

I'm no longer keeping those running shoes in my closet. I'm sitting still. Ten toes down! And you should do the same too.

I heard the bar for love is somewhere in hell these days but what if your person is standing *right outside the gate*, waiting to help you walk back up to heaven?

Sis, Don't Block Your Blessing. Please.

Sis, it's time to start praying and believing that God sends you everything you've asked for:
The job.
The man.
The friendships.
The open doors.

But you can't pray in fear and receive in doubt.

SIS, ARE YOU BLOCKING YOUR OWN BLESSINGS?

You have to stop questioning whether you deserve it and start preparing to hold it.

As I reflect on my journey and walk beside you through yours, let me be clear. I'm not an expert, but I've lived. I've made mistakes, sabotaged good things, ignored red flags, and even ran from green ones.

And guess what? I'm still here. Stronger. Softer. Wiser.
You can be vulnerable and still be powerful. You can express your feelings and *still* hold your boundaries.
You can feel deeply without losing yourself.

And if we're talking examples? Let's talk about Ruth!

Ruth wasn't out there, doing backflips to catch Boaz's attention.
Sis wasn't sliding into DMs, (not that DMs was around then) but she wasn't performing for love. She was just handling her business.

In position. In purpose. In peace.

And Boaz saw her.
Not because she forced it.
But because alignment always attracts the right eyes. Let that sink in.

You don't have to chase love. Be Ruth. Do your work. Stay in purpose. Let love find you in the field.

Sis, the world is wide open in front of you. Don't just be fixated on one slice and miss the whole feast God's laid out for you. And don't use one or two bad experience to dictate how the future will be.

The love you want. It'll find you. The partnership you desire? It'll meet you right where you are. You *will* be chosen. You *will* be cherished.

SIS, YOU ARE HER

Just don't run when it shows up.

But until then? **LIFE GOES ON....**

Sis, you are not alone, and you'll realize this in the next chapter.

HER Mirror Moment: Sis, Say It Out Loud

"I am not my family. I am not what they endured. I am no longer self-sabotaging. I am not running. I am Her. I am capable of love, and I will not run from it when it finally shows up."

HER Word: Sis, Let's Reflect

This is your moment. Grab your *"Her Reflection"* journal, find a quiet space, and give yourself the gift of honesty. These questions aren't just here to be read, they're here to help you grow.

Take your time. Be real. Be gentle.
You're not just writing. You are healing.

Your Reflection Questions

1. In what ways have you been pushing away the very things you've prayed for?
2. What fear is driving your desire to stay in control?
3. What would it feel like to be loved without shrinking, hiding, or overthinking?
4. Is there any part of you that believes you're not ready, or not enough, for the blessing you asked for?

3

SIS, YOU ARE NOT ALONE

*"You're not the only one who's ever stayed too long, questioned
her worth, or lost herself trying to be enough. You're not
broken; you're just healing."*

— Yanique P. Walters

S is, let's shift gears and talk about something important: **US**! It's easy
to start thinking that everyone else has it all figured out and it's just
you, but I need you to know that you are not the only one who's
ever felt lost, questioned her worth, or stayed longer than she should've.
I surveyed women just like you — different ages, backgrounds, and
stories, about what they've struggled with most when it comes to love,
confidence, and healing.

When I put out the survey asking women to share their hearts, I honestly didn't know what to expect. I figured a few brave souls would answer. But the outcome I got, whew. Sis, it was like opening a floodgate of honesty, pain, dreams, regrets, and hope.

I cried reading those stories. Because in every line, I saw a piece of me. And maybe, you'll see a piece of you too.

The area most of us are struggling with includes confessions like:

- "I always give great advice, but I never follow it for myself."
- "I stayed because I thought no one else would want me."
- "I didn't know if I'd be anything without him. That scared me more than being unhappy."
- "I thought if I loved him hard enough, he'd change."
- "I can't tell if I'm healing or just learning how to hide the hurt better."
- "I'm tired of being strong. I just want to feel soft and safe."
- "I stayed because of the financial benefits — I wasn't independent enough to leave. I needed financial security."

Sis… if any of these sounds like you, then let's dive into the survey.

Confidence — Where It Really Stands

When asked about their confidence, most women rated themselves somewhere in the middle, not low, but not fully where they want to be either. A few said they were thriving in their confidence, but many admitted it still wavers, depending on how life and love are treating them.

Sis, confidence isn't a destination. It's a daily decision. It's not about "arriving" and never doubting yourself again. It's about waking up each day, even on the messy days, and choosing to believe in your own magic. As you read earlier, I gained mine then lost it again.

> *Sisterly Advice:*
> *There will be days you feel unstoppable and days you feel unseen.*
> *Both days are valid.*
> *But neither day defines your worth.*
>
> *Don't beat yourself up.*
> *Don't talk yourself out of your own greatness.*
> *Better days are ahead, and confidence can always be rebuilt, restored, and renewed.*

Validation — The Silent Thief

I asked women why they seek validation from unavailable men. Sis… the answers came pouring in—raw, vulnerable, and heartbreaking. Some said they were raised in environments where love was conditional. Others said they didn't feel beautiful or wanted while growing up, so any attention at all felt like oxygen. Some said when a man chooses you, it feels like a proof that you're enough.

Others said they stayed because they didn't want to start over, or they hoped they could finally "win" love where it's hard. Many shared that deep down, they believed they had to earn love—to prove themselves lovable by fixing, healing, or saving broken people. While themselves are broken, forgetting that broken people break others. And the cycle continues like a ripple effect.

And Sis, I get it. I've been there too, thinking if I just loved harder, waited longer, became better, or maybe just fixed him… then maybe they'd finally choose me.

Reading those responses reminded me: sometimes we chase people who reject us because it mirrors the wounds we haven't healed from. We'll dive deeper into trauma in Chapter 4.

Sisterly Advice:
Validation that you have to beg for isn't validation, it's manipulation. The right kind of love feels like a mirror, not a maze. You shouldn't have to audition for love.

Self-Worth — The Root of It All

I asked what affects self-worth the most, and Sis, the patterns were clear: failed relationships, rejection, betrayal, family wounds, childhood neglect, social media comparisons. It wasn't just romantic failures—it was years of invisible wounds stacking on top of each other. It was being told, directly or indirectly, that we had to shrink, to settle, to "be realistic" about what we could hope for.

Specifically, what affects their self-worth the most, were:

- Being mistreated in relationships
- Comparing themselves to other women
- Childhood wounds that were never healed
- Feeling unseen or undervalued by family or partners

Reading those responses felt like sitting at a kitchen table with my sisters, sharing stories of hurt, betrayal, and survival. And through it all, one thing became crystal clear: our self-worth often takes the deepest hits from the places we expected to feel safest. Cliché, but true.

And that's why healing has to start with us. Not with them. Not with getting closure. Not with proving anything to anybody.

Sisterly Advice:
Self-worth isn't about who chooses you.
It's about who you choose to be—with or without applause.

The Regret That Echoed

When women explained why they stayed in relationships that no longer served them, the answers were heartbreaking—but came from places of hope, fear, loyalty, and sometimes survival. It was all about seeing the red flags and consciously choosing to ignore them. I wanted to know why.

While some stayed because they remembered the man he used to be, some stayed because leaving meant facing loneliness. And others stayed because they thought he would change if they loved him enough.

One thing that echoed loudly was: *"I knew better, but I thought he would change."*

Sis, how many times have we displayed the same patterns? How many times have we bet on someone's potential instead of accepting their reality? Hope is beautiful, but misplaced hope will bleed you dry.

Sisterly Advice:
Sis, staying in a place that keeps hurting you doesn't mean you're loyal. It means you're still learning how to love yourself more than you love the idea of potential. Red flags don't turn green over time. They become intensified. Love isn't built on potential; it's built on patterns.

Sis, if you recognized yourself in these stories, hear me clearly: **you're not broken. You're not foolish. You're not weak.** You're just human. A beautiful, large-hearted, healing human who is learning to honor her worth in a world that tries to rob her of it.

This chapter is your reminder that you're not crazy for wanting more, and you're not asking for too much. You're simply asking the wrong people to give you what they're not capable of giving.

I see how much you want to believe the best in people. How you give them so much grace, yet they reject you. And Sis, that's beautiful. That's not something you need to change. You don't need to love less; you just need to love **wiser**. And that's what this journey is about.

So, take a deep breath, give yourself grace, and keep going. Now, let's discuss some of those traumas and how they affect us in the next chapter.

HER Mirror Moment: Sis, Say It Out Loud

"I am not alone in this journey. My story is valid, my healing is sacred, and I am worthy of love, peace, and soft spaces. I give myself permission to grow, to feel, and to be seen."

HER Word: Sis, Let's Reflect

Now Sis, grab your journal—yes, your *"Her Reflection"* journal, and let's go inward for a moment. Write freely. No filters. This space is for you.

Your Reflection Questions

1. What part of the survey responses got you saying, *"Wow... that's me"*?
2. How have you felt seen or unseen in your relationships, and what do you want to change about that going forward?
3. What's one promise you're ready to make to yourself, starting today?
4. Who or what has made you feel most seen during your lowest moments and how can you remind yourself of that support?

4

SIS, HEALING IS MESSY, BUT WORTH IT

"Healing isn't always pretty, but it's holy. It's the quiet
rebellion of choosing yourself after generations of survival."

— *Yanique P. Walters*

S is, it's about to get real here. This is probably one of those topics we hate to talk about or worse, our parents hate to hear about. Like, what do you mean you have trauma? My mom would say, "Why are you picking up this "American culture"?" But sis, we need to talk about it, so get a glass of wine and get comfy.

Generational Silence and Strength

As Black people, our history is rooted in survival. From slavery to segregation, we've been taught to be strong, to push through, to keep moving no matter the weight we carry. For generations, silence was strength, and emotions were tucked away. Growing up, the word "trauma" didn't exist in my vocabulary unless we were talking about a blow to the head, not funny, but true.

Understanding Trauma

But trauma is deeper than that. Let me define it for the people in the back: Trauma is a deeply distressing or disturbing experience that overwhelms your ability to cope. It can stem from a single event or a series of events and often leaves a lasting impact on your emotional, mental, or physical well-being. Trauma isn't just about what happened. It's about how your mind, body, and spirit responded to what happened. And what feels traumatic to one person may not feel the same to another. Because trauma is personal. It lives in your nervous system, not just your memory.

Recognizing Trauma Responses

A lot of what we do is our body responding to trauma, trying to keep us safe. I'll be honest: I've seen a lot in my life. So much so that sometimes I would find myself living on edge, always waiting for the next bad thing to happen. I used to trust people up front... until something triggered me. Then that trust disappeared. That's a trauma response. And it wasn't until I slowed down and got curious about my own patterns that I realized it.

Her Story, Our Mirror

In one of the surveys I conducted for this book, a sister shared her story, and sis, it stayed with me:

I never thought I'd be the kind of woman who stayed with someone who didn't treat her right. I was strong. Independent. I was taught to never settle for less. But somehow, I found myself loving a man who broke me in ways I didn't know I could be broken.

In the beginning, he was everything I thought I wanted - charming, attentive, protective. He'd text me every morning just to say he missed me. He remembered my favorite snacks, opened doors, and made me feel like the only woman in the world. It felt like a dream. But looking back, I realize that dream started to feel more like a trap.

The red flags came slowly. At first, it was the way he questioned what I wore. Then, the way he'd get upset if I didn't answer the phone fast enough. I told myself it was just because he cared. He said he just didn't want to lose me, and that he had 'been through things'. And I believed him.

I stayed through the mood swings, the silent treatments, the guilt trips. I started walking on eggshells just to keep the peace. I'd convince myself that he was just stressed, or that maybe I was overreacting. I held onto the good moments like they were gold, ignoring the growing pile of bad ones.

Why didn't I leave? Because I kept hoping he'd go back to the man I met in the beginning. Because he'd say sorry with tears in his eyes and a promise to be better. Because he'd talk about our future like we still had one. And maybe, deep down, I thought I could love him into healing.

I felt ashamed to tell anyone. I didn't want to be judged for staying. I didn't want to hear 'I told you so'. So I kept it to myself, until one day I couldn't anymore. I was tired. Tired of pretending. Tired of feeling numb.

It took time, and support, and a lot of self-forgiveness. But I eventually walked away. And in doing so, I learned that love should never make you feel small, scared, or silenced.

So when people ask, 'Why do women stay?' I say because we're human. Because sometimes love blinds us. Because we're hopeful. Because the heart isn't logical, especially when it's attached to a memory of what once was.

But we also leave. When we're ready. When we remember who we are. And that's what matters most.

Reading this with an untrained eye, even I could identify the trauma within her story: the people-pleasing, the guilt, the shame, the gaslighting, the silence. But what gave me hope was her self-awareness. And that, sis, is the beginning of healing.

Unpacking Childhood and Cultural Trauma

See, trauma doesn't always start in adulthood. It can start way back from childhood. A parent who criticized you. A parent who was absent. Words that got spoken over you that you never shook off. Parents being divorced. Medical issues that you encountered. Someone you expected to have your back but didn't. Abuse by family members or people close to you. Sexual molestation by an uncle or an older person who ought to have protected you but took advantage of you instead.

Not all trauma looks the same. Some of us walked through hell and didn't even realize it because we were too busy surviving.

When Strength Is a Survival Mask

At 16, I was raising my siblings, ages 13, 10, and 2, while my mom worked overseas to provide for us. Being Jamaican, I didn't see it as trauma. I saw it as a duty. As what needed to be done. I was the oldest, and I had to assist my mom. No questions asked.

Even now, I still hesitate to call it trauma. But when I share that story, people look at me with pity. They say things like, "Wow… that must've been so hard." And maybe it was. It made me grow up fast. But that maturity has sometimes worked against me, I'll explain more in the later chapters. But I am grateful for that chapter of my life.

Hidden Trauma, Daily Triggers

What I've come to realize is: trauma doesn't always come with bruises or loud cries. Sometimes, it shows up quietly… like when I needed help with my own child and no one showed up for me.

That moment when I think, Dang, I bent over backwards for everybody… but where's that same love for me?

I didn't expect payback. I did it out of the goodness of my heart. But that's the tricky thing about trauma, it lives in the mind like saved data. One moment triggers another. Suddenly, your brain starts comparing, calculating, and asking questions you didn't even know existed in your sub-consciousness.

Types of Traumas

Let's name a few types of traumas, so you can recognize it if it happens to show up in your life:

Acute Trauma - This comes from a single, stressful or dangerous event. It can be that breakup that shattered your world. The day you found out about the betrayal. The loss that hit you out of nowhere.

Chronic Trauma - This is the kind that builds over time, constant criticism growing up, repeated rejection, being in an emotionally or physically abusive relationship, or even long-term financial instability.

Complex Trauma - Whew! This one's layered. It stems from multiple or prolonged events, especially in childhood—like neglect, abandonment, or exposure to chaos.

Generational Trauma - Some of the things you carry didn't even start with you. Generational trauma gets passed down through behaviors, beliefs, silence.

Relational Trauma -This comes from betrayal or damage in close relationships. Maybe you trusted someone with your heart, and they mishandled it.

Naming What Hurts

Sis, I know this might feel heavy. But identifying the type of trauma you've experienced is powerful. Because how can you heal from something you can't name?

Here's what I want you to know: Trauma might protect you, but it also limits you. It keeps you from walking into rooms where you belong. It convinces you that you're not good enough. It tells you not to trust love. It makes you sabotage the very thing you prayed for. Yep, you don't want to do that!

How Trauma Distorts Love

I was the queen of self-sabotage. Chile! I would walk away from a good man before he had the chance to walk away from me. But I know I am not the only one. Let me tell you about a client...

She met an amazing man; he was doing everything right but in the back of her mind she wondered. She'd ask, "Is he only doing this because he wants a green card?" Because sis, when trauma is your compass, even love feels like a trap. Constantly needed reassurance.

That's how trauma works. It builds walls around your heart and then dares anyone to climb them. But here's the thing: those walls don't just keep pain out; they keep love out too.

Patterns We Inherit

Some of your trauma might be inherited. I know mine was. My mother struggled with her own pain. This resulted in her comparing me to others, made me question my worth, and unintentionally planted seeds of doubt in me. I watched her give her all to men who did her wrong, and I told myself: that will never be me. Deep down I know she meant well for me, but the seed was already planted so it materialized into my own relationships because at the first sign of anything that looks like what the men in my mom's life possess, I am out. It took therapy for me to realize what was happening. Our parents aren't perfect people; they too were trying to figure life out and sometimes they unintentional plant seeds in us. Don't be too hard on them.

Let me leave you with this:

> *"If you don't heal from what hurt you, you'll bleed on people who didn't cut you."* —**Unknown**

And another one that stays with me:

> *"You can't heal in the same environment that broke you."*
> — *Anonymous*

Sis… you deserve to feel safe. To feel whole. To feel free.

Healing might not be a straight line, but it's real. And it's possible. One step, one truth, one journal page at a time.

The Healing Movement — and Why It Matters Now
Healing is what sharpens your intuition.
Healing is what clears the noise.
Healing is what helps you distinguish fear from discernment.

A healed spirit can hear God clearly. A wounded spirit often only hears anxiety.

Healing doesn't mean forgetting.
Healing doesn't mean pretending it never happened.
Healing doesn't mean the pain disappears overnight.

Healing means:

- You don't repeat the lesson
- You don't betray yourself again
- You don't ignore your spirit
- You choose peace instead of potential

Healing is a redirection — a recalibration of your spirit.
It turns chaos into clarity.
It turns confusion into discernment.
It turns wounds into wisdom.

And when you heal? Sis… everything shifts.

You stop chasing clarity from people who thrive in confusion.
You stop doubting God's warnings.
You stop silencing the nudge in your belly.
You stop betraying yourself to feel chosen.

Healing helps you trust **YOU** again.

The next time you start to question whether you want to take the time to heal or not, remember the above.

In the next chapter, we're uncovering some layers. We're examining the people in your life—the ones who are truly showing up for you and those just hanging around. Because let's be clear: your healing doesn't need an audience; it needs protection.

So, take a moment. Pause. Breathe. Get honest.

Write it out, what hurts you, what still lingers, what you haven't said out loud yet. Name it, sis. That's how we start to release it.

And if you're holding pain that feels too heavy to journal through… consider therapy. That's not weakness, it's wisdom. It's saying: *I love myself enough to be carrying this alone.*

Are you ready? Let's go!

HER Mirror Moment: Sis, Say It Out Loud

"I am not my trauma. I am healing. I am growing. I deserve peace, love, and safety in every part of my life."

HER Word: Sis, Let's Reflect

But before we go there, grab your *"Her Reflection"* journal. Yes, Sis, we're now in Chapter 4, and if you haven't gotten yours yet, this is your sign. It's time to get real about your trauma. And writing it out? That's where the shift begins. We're doing the work, sis. And the woman you're becoming? She's worth it

Your Reflection Questions:

1. What past experience(s) still triggers an emotional reaction in you?
2. What beliefs do you carry that may have come from someone else's pain?
3. In what areas of your life are you still moving from a place of protection instead of peace?
4. What would giving yourself permission to fully feel, without rushing to fix it, look like right now?

5

SIS, KNOW WHO'S SITTING AT YOUR TABLE

"The deepest cuts don't come from strangers; they come from
the hands we once held in trust. But Sis, your healing begins
the moment you stop calling betrayal love."
— Yanique P. Walters

S is, in the last chapter we talked about trauma. And if we're being honest, some of the people who caused the deepest trauma in our lives are still around us. It's tough, especially when it wasn't always intentional. Sometimes they hurt us in the only way they knew how to love. But even if they didn't mean harm, the pain still lingers.

You don't have to carry anger, but you also don't have to stay silent. You can name what happened. And you can choose how close those people get to your heart from here onward. We'll talk more about boundaries soon but know this now: you're allowed to protect your peace, even from people you love.

Your Enemy May Be Closer Than You Think

Sometimes the person who's hurting you is the one you least expect. A best friend. A cousin. A mentor. Even a sibling. And it's hard, because we want to believe that the people we trust are rooting for us. We want to hear them shouting our names from the back of the room, but that's not always the case, sometimes they are secretly envious.

Let me tell you a story about a true betrayal. I once had a man who was interested in me. I wasn't completely sure about him, but I was open. He came to visit me in Jamaica from overseas, and during his trip, I invited my close friend and her son to join us at the beach. I genuinely wanted them to enjoy the day with us.

While her son and my guy were out in the water, I opened up to her. I shared that he wanted to marry me, but I wasn't certain. It was still early, and there were things I wasn't fully settled about.

What I didn't expect was for her to take what I said and use it as an opening. She reached out to him on Skype later, flirted with him, and told him I wasn't that into him. What she didn't expect was that he was going to come back and tell me everything! She thought she was doing him a favor, Chile!

I would be lying if I said that it didn't hurt deeply. This wasn't just some girl; I brought her into my space, shared food, shared trust, and shared my thoughts. And she violated all of that. For what? The thought of moving to the US? I honestly didn't see that coming. I couldn't see her the same way anymore, so I ended the friendship. Years had gone by until we finally spoke again. I had already made peace with what happened. I forgave her, but things weren't going to go back to the way it was before.

That's the thing about betrayal: it shifts something in you. You see people differently. And sometimes the hardest part isn't what they did, it's that you didn't expect it from them.

Stop Ignoring the Red Flags

Sis, there's danger in constantly brushing off the red flags and it's something that we do way too often. We feel the energy shift. We hear the off comments. We perceive the jealousy. But we don't want to believe it's real. So, we silence our intuition until the truth is too loud to ignore.

The reality is, betrayal will continue to happen. Betrayal isn't new, it's ancient. Jealousy, betrayal, envy from those closest to you has been happening since the beginning of time.

Cain and Abel were the very first siblings. Two brothers — one's offering was accepted, and the other's was rejected. Cain couldn't handle the perceived rejection. Instead of learning from it or searching within, he let jealousy grow until it turned into rage. He killed his own brother. Not a stranger, his brother.

Joseph was betrayed by his brothers not because he wronged them, but because he was favored. Because he dreamed. Because he was different. And they couldn't take it. So, they stripped him, threw him in a pit, and sold him. They lied to their father. They watched their own brother suffer just to feel better about themselves.

David and Saul, this one hit differently. David served Saul. Protected him. Brought peace to his tormented spirit. But when David's light started shining a little too bright, when the praise got louder, Saul let jealousy ruin what could've been a powerful partnership. He went from loving David to plotting his death.

Jesus and Judas – this one is the reason we are all here.

The pattern is clear: betrayal doesn't usually come from far away. It often comes from within, from people who have your number saved in their phone, from the ones you call family, from those you thought would never hurt you.

As Bob Marley once said:

> *"Your worst enemy could be your best friend, and your best friend your worst enemy."*

Because only your best friend knows your secrets. And when envy takes root, those secrets become weapons.

I remember attending *Tonight's Conversation*, a podcast aimed at answering real dating and relationship questions. A woman stood up, and with pain in her voice asked:

> *"How do I move forward in my marriage when my husband had an affair with my sister?"*

Sis, the air left the room.

You could feel everyone's heart break just a little for her. Because that wasn't just infidelity. That was betrayal on both sides; by the man who vowed to love her and the sister she likely grew up protecting, laughing with, venting to. The betrayal wasn't just physical; it was emotional, spiritual, and psychological.

So How Do You Move Forward?

There's no one-size-fits-all answer to that level of pain. Healing from that kind of betrayal requires a full reset. Not just of the relationship, but of your heart, your boundaries, and your sense of self. Some people try to stay, hoping love can rewrite the story. Others have to walk away, not because they didn't love, but because they refused to keep bleeding in silence.

If that kind of wound is ever going to heal, then it starts with the truth. Everyone involved has to take accountability. There has to be honesty, deep therapy, spiritual grounding, and time — lots of time.

And for the person who was betrayed? You have to give yourself permission to feel everything. The rage. The sadness. The numbness. And then, when you're ready, you decide: What does healing look like?
Not for marriage.
Not for the sister.
Not for what people think you should do.
But for you.

And sometimes, Sis, healing looks like walking away with your dignity intact. With your head high. With your soul still whole.

Here's How You Start Healing and Protecting Your Peace

1. **Acknowledge what happened.**
   Stop excusing or making excuses for their (terrible) behavior just because you love them. Your pain is valid.

2. **Protect your peace.**
   Distance is not bitterness. It's wisdom. Forgiveness doesn't mean reconnection.

3. **Trust your intuition.**
   You felt it. That uneasiness wasn't just in your head. Start trusting that inner voice again.

4. **Redefine your circle.**
   People who celebrate your wins, not compete with them. People who hold your secrets, not use them. That's who belongs close.

5. **Ask God for discernment.**
   Not just for the snakes, but for the silent envy. For the ones who smile but hope you fall.

Jealousy, when left unchecked, turns into destruction. And it often comes from those close enough to study your light and secretly resent it. But Sis, even when they try to bury you, God still has a plan to raise you up. Let your healing begin with truth. Let your discernment be sharper. And let your boundaries be stronger.

You're not bitter.

You're just finally paying attention.

Now that we have completed part one, let's jump into part two and talk about confidence! We all need this.

But before we move on, sis, take a moment. Breathe. You've just read some heavy truth, and it's okay if it stirred something in you. If you've ever been betrayed by someone close, I want you to know you're not alone.

HER Mirror Moment: Sis, Say It Out Loud

"I am worthy of loyalty, honesty, and peace. I will no longer make excuses for those who hurt me. I protect my heart without apology."

HER Word: Sis, Let's Reflect

This is the part where you grab your *"Her Reflection"* journal. Not to write the perfect words, but to be honest. Raw. Unfiltered. Because healing doesn't come from hiding your pain, it comes from facing it. So go ahead. Sit with what you feel. Let it spill onto the page. Let it release from your chest

Your Reflection Questions:

1. Have you ever ignored red flags because you didn't want to lose someone you loved?
2. What did that betrayal teach you about myself? And how can you honor that lesson moving forward?
3. Who in your life do you need to create emotional distance from to protect your peace?
4. In what ways have you kept people close out of strategy, fear, or habit, when they've already shown you who they are?

SIS, HERE'S THE TRUTH I HAD TO LEARN

Sis, after reading PART 1, I hope you have noted down things you wish you knew. These are the things I wish I knew, so that I wouldn't have made certain mistakes.

Chapter 1: Sis, The Mirror Doesn't Lie

- Just because you're showing up every day doesn't mean you're okay. And that's not weakness, that's real.
- The version of you that felt fearless and joyful still exists underneath the pain.
- You don't have to earn rest, softness, or self-compassion.
- Survival is not your personality. You were made for more – more than just getting through the day.
- Strength isn't only found in pushing through, it's found in honoring your needs too.

Chapter 2: Sis, Are You Blocking Your Blessings

- If you don't believe you're worthy, you'll mistrust anything that feels good.
- You attract who you are - heal from your past hurt, so you can attract and keep only that which is as authentic as you.
- Real love won't feel like performing, proving, or pleasing.
- Avoidance isn't always wisdom, sometimes it's fear in disguise.
- Healthy love may feel boring at first if chaos is all you've known.
- Healing your nervous system – your mental self, is just as important as healing your heart.

Chapter 3: Sis, You are Not Alone

- Being the strong one doesn't mean you don't need support.
- Silence can be heavy. Your story deserves to breathe, it deserves to be heard.
- You're not crazy. You're not the only one. You're not too much.
- When you speak your truth, you give others permission to do the same.
- Vulnerability builds bridges, shame builds walls.
- God never meant for you to carry this all by yourself.

Chapter 4: Sis, Healing Is Messy, But Worth It

- There's no "arrival" point in healing, it's a journey, not a destination.
- One bad day doesn't mean you've failed.
- Healing might cost you relationships that were built on your brokenness.
- You'll have days when you miss what hurt you, and that's normal.
- Progress often feels invisible, but it's still progress.
- You're allowed to celebrate small wins because they matter. They're the building blocks of "big" wins.

Chapter 5: Sis, Keep Your Enemies Closer

- Just because someone is close to you doesn't mean they're rooting for you.
- Loyalty should be mutual. Stop giving yours to people who weaponize it against you.

- Peace is a form of discernment—listen when your spirit feels uneasy.
- You don't have to confront everyone. Distance is a decision, not drama.
- God will reveal what needs to be revealed in His time. You don't need to force it.

PART TWO

Sis, Build from the Inside Out

This is where we talk about the experiences that shaped you.

6

SIS, LET'S TALK CONFIDENCE

"I wore the heels before I felt tall, spoke the truth before I felt brave, and that's how I became her — confident, whole, and unshaken."
— Yanique P. Walters

C an I be real with you for a second? A few years ago, a group of women I thought I connected with got together, but I wasn't invited.

And it stung. Because even as grown women, that feeling of being left out cuts deep. You start asking yourself, *what's wrong with me? Why don't I fit in? Did I say something? Did I do something?*

But here's what I'm learning, sis: sometimes the answer isn't about us at all. Sometimes people don't include you because of their own cliques, their own dynamics, and their own insecurities. And sometimes, it's simply because your presence doesn't fit the room God never meant for you to stay in. Heck... I learned that its ok to standout, we don't have to always force ourselves to fit in.

So instead of spiraling into *what's wrong with me,* I'm shifting the question to *what about me isn't for them?* Because the truth is, being excluded is painful—but it's also redirection. It's God whispering, *'Don't waste energy fighting to belong where I never called you.'*

Sis, if you've ever been left out, ignored, or overlooked, you're not alone. I've been there too. But I promise you this: the right tables will never require you to beg for a chair. The right sisterhood will see your light and say, *'Come sit with us—we've been waiting on you.*

And here's the truth: moments like this don't just bruise your feelings, they chip away at your confidence. They make you question your worth, your value, your place.

So, Sis, Let's Talk Confidence

We are going to dive into self-confidence, self-worth, self-esteem, and self-value. Because truthfully? This is where it begins. If we had all four in check, half of the things we tolerate in relationships, friendships, and even careers would be non-existent.

Know the Difference

Let's start by understanding the difference between them, because they're not interchangeable.

Self-confidence is your belief in your ability to do something.

Self-worth is the inner knowing that you are inherently deserving of love, respect, and goodness, regardless of what you've achieved. Regardless of how ugly your past may be.

Self-esteem is how you feel about yourself overall, based on your life experiences and inner voice. It is how you carry yourself.

Self-value is how you honor that worth in your decisions, your boundaries, and the energy you allow into your space.

Think of it like this:

- **Self-confidence** says, "I can."

- **Self-worth** says, "I am enough."

- **Self-esteem** says, "I feel good about who I am."

- **Self-value** says, "I refuse to settle for less."

Now that we've got that covered, let's dig deeper. When I asked women in the survey what affects their self-worth and confidence the most, the answers hit hard — relationships, body image, finances, comparison on social media, childhood trauma, unhealed wounds, not keeping boundaries and the list goes on. And Sis, I get it. I've lived it too.

My Personal Battle With Beauty

I struggled for years believing I wasn't worthy of real love. I grew up being teased relentlessly about how I looked. They called me "Nanny Buck Buck" because of my forehead, "dry-head gal" because of my hair texture, and "big mouth girl" for the size of my lips. But the one insult that cut the deepest was, "ugly." That one stuck. For years, I believed it.

Any time someone I liked chose another girl, especially one I deemed more "attractive," I told myself it was because I wasn't pretty enough.

The Shift: Taking My Power Back
I told the story about when I felt something in me shift. I decided it was time to take my power back. I looked in the mirror and said, "You're about to be sick of me." I started seeing myself the way God saw me. I stopped shrinking. And you know what changed? Not my face. Not my body. But my belief. I finally saw myself through God's lenses, not my own eyes, not theirs. I shifted my **MINDSET**. I reminded myself daily how beautiful I was.

That was the start of my I AM THAT GIRL era.

"I Cared Zero"

For a while, I made it my mission to care less about what others thought. I even had a motto: "I care zero." I conditioned myself to care only about the opinion of God and myself, because the truth is, I'm not here to impress men, strangers, or anyone who doesn't feed my purpose.

Sis, I've Been There Too
Sis, when I talk about confidence, know that I'm not speaking from some high pedestal. I've been at rock bottom. I've stood before the mirror and hated what I saw. I let old voices and fresh doubts convince me I wasn't enough. But I fought my way back. And if I could do it, you can too.

The Blue Ivy Effect
Let's talk about someone who was publicly torn down from a young age—Blue Ivy. From the moment she was born, people called her ugly. They talked about how much she looked like her dad and not enough

like Beyoncé. And it didn't stop there. When she first hit the stage dancing, the internet was brutal.

But imagine if she had believed all that. Imagine if she didn't have a strong support system.

She didn't let anything the naysayers had to say stop her. The people in her corner kept her protected.

She came back the following year, stronger, sharper, more confident. And now? The same people who doubted her are saying, "Wow, she's killing it!"

That's what belief and resilience can do.

From Doubt to Testimony

Sis, your story can shift too. With faith, practice, and self-belief, your "they doubted me" moment can turn into a "look at me now" testimony.

Here's what I've learned along the way: if people don't see something in you to envy or admire, they won't even acknowledge you. And if they don't have what it takes to compete with you, they'll compare you to someone else just to dim your light.

But here's the truth:

> *People don't throw shade at what's in the dark. They only shade what shines. If you are being attacked, just know it's because you are shining.*

Don't Let Instagram Fool You

Let's shift gear and talk about social media. I know you see the girls on Instagram with flawless makeup, snatched bodies, perfect boyfriends, and luxury vacations. But Sis, most of it is smoke and mirrors. You don't know the fire giving off the smoke, nor the real object before the mirror.

Confidence is not loud lashes and designer bags. Confidence is how you talk to yourself when no one else is hyping you up. It's showing up when you don't feel ready. It's knowing you're the prize, even when no one is clapping.

Behind the Scenes Ain't Always Pretty

One time, a man slid into my DMs while parading his fiancée on his page like a queen. Yet here he was, chasing me behind the scenes. That's when it clicked: don't judge your worth based on someone else's highlight reel. A man once told me he only posts his wife so she can feel special, but he'll be doing his thing.

Sir, what?

But here we are, praising them for being the power couple we desire to be.

From the Mouths of Men

Anyways, let me bring in one of the men's survey responses that hit hard. When asked what he does if a woman shows signs of low confidence in a relationship, he said:

"If it started during our time together, I'm invested in helping. But if it comes from past relationships and she won't let go of those voices, I eventually leave. If her ex told her she can't cook and she believes it, how can I help her believe otherwise? I've been with women who couldn't accept my compliments because they held onto their ex's opinion. And it got exhausting."

Whew. That one stung a little. Because I've been her.

Another guy said, that's his type of woman. Women with insecurity issues are easy targets.

That one stopped me in my tracks. Jaws dropped and all.

You've Got to Heal, Sis
We can't drag the pain of our exes into the presence of someone trying to love us. You have to heal before you bleed all over someone who didn't cut you.

When I Doubted My Voice
Another area where I doubted myself? Speaking. But I kept showing up anyway. I reminded myself, "I belong here. I have value. I bring something to the table." I told myself, "Even if I'm scared, I'll do it anyway." And Sis, that's the definition of courage—feeling fear and doing it anyway.

Strong on the Outside, Breaking on the Inside
Lack of confidence spills into every area—relationships, work, self-worth. I avoided eye contact. No one really knew how much I was struggling.

Because I was "the strong one."

Ladies, check on your strong friends. They battle so much daily, that no one ever thinks to ask the four -words question, "How are you really"?

The Cry That Set Me Free
It took breaking down at work. In front of my leader. To realize how much I was hurting. But that cry? It helped.

I made me realize I needed to put in the work. And I did.

Purpose in the Pain

I started journaling, just to get my mind right. That turned into a gratitude journal I published. The leadership team gifted it to the entire team of over 300 staff; I'll tell you about that later.

But it shows that even in my chaos—I was making an impact. And if no one knew, no impact would have been made.

The Price of Confidence

Here's the kicker: once I became this confident version of myself, men got intimidated.

Some said, "You look too expensive." Others said, "I'm shocked you'd talk to someone like me."

And Sis, while I'm not doing this for them, it does feel good to know my energy says: "Don't you dare play with me."

Stop Shrinking for His Comfort

Sis, take your notebook and write this down:

- If a man doesn't believe he has the capacity to date you, don't force it.
- If he can't recognize your value, don't explain it.
- If he calls you "too much," trust that he's just not enough.

A Bold Woman's Words

One woman said in the survey:

"I command the respect I desire… I de-center men… I'm not friends with any woman who prioritizes men or makes her whole life about keeping one."

Whether you agree with her or not, **that kind of self-centered power is what builds unshakable confidence.**

You Are the Constant
Sis, don't tie your worth to how well you show up for others. Because if they stop seeing your value, you'll question if you have any.

And yes, you do. You always have. So, we need to avoid that feeling at all costs.

Now Sis, Let's Start Somewhere

Building confidence takes time. But here's what helped me:

- **Dress the Way You Want to Be Addressed**
  Stop waiting to lose weight. Wear the heels. Walk with your head high. Wear whatever the heck you want to.
- **Speak Kindly to Yourself**
  Your mind is always listening. Watch how you talk about yourself.
- **Journal Your Wins**
  Celebrate even the small wins. Remind yourself that you're making progress.
- **Unfollow the Noise**
  Protect your peace. Mute or unfollow anyone and anything that disrupts it.
- **Show Up for You**
  Take the trip. Book the class. Keep promises to yourself.
- **Set Boundaries**
  "No" is a full sentence. Boundaries are filters, not walls.

- **Affirm Yourself**
  Even if your voice shakes. Say it:
  "I am worthy. I am enough. I am growing. I am becoming"
- **Do It Scared**
  I joined Toastmasters. I posted videos. I did it fearfully. Confidence is built through action.
- **Prioritize Yourself first**

Girl, stop putting everyone and everything before you.

Sis, You Are Enough

Every time you choose yourself, you're building - brick by brick. You don't need to be loud to be powerful. The loudest person is not always the most confident. You don't have to wait to be perfect before you can see your worth. Just be committed to your healing.

We are at the end of another powerful chapter, but we are going to keep going. Next, we're going to talk about boundaries—because sis, who do they think they are, and why do they believe they can play with you?

Confidence sounds simple on paper — but the real work begins when you start examining *why* you lost it in the first place. Confidence doesn't disappear overnight; it's chipped away through experiences, environments, and moments that made you question who you are and how you show up. And for many of us, it wasn't that we lacked confidence... it's that we were put in spaces that made us doubt our wiring. Before we talk about boundaries, love, self-care, or anything else, we need to address one of the biggest roots of broken confidence: **feeling misunderstood.**

So sis, let's go there.

HER Mirror Moment: Sis, Say It Out Loud

"I was created with purpose.
I walk in rooms like I belong there—because I do.
I am not shrinking anymore.
This light is meant to shine."

HER Word: Sis, Let's Reflect

Before we move on, grab your journal. These questions are here to help you see how powerful you already are.

Your Reflection Questions

1. What lies have you believed about yourself? What truths do you need to start speaking?
2. When was the last time you felt truly confident? What contributed to it?
3. Where do you still second-guess yourself, and why?
4. If you showed up as the most confident version of myself tomorrow, how would you speak, move, and decide?

7

SIS, YOU'RE NOT DIFFICULT, YOU'RE MISUNDERSTOOD

"Once you understand your own wiring, you stop apologizing for the woman God designed on purpose.

— Yanique P. Walters

S is, I recently had a conversation with a friend who told me she had a disagreement with the people closest to her. She said they weren't listening, weren't seeing her heart, weren't understanding her intentions. They painted her based on a moment instead of her character. This is someone who considers herself very predictable and believes those closest to her will always know her heart and know what she will and will not do.

She said something that hit me deep: **"I just felt misunderstood."**
Not wrong.
Not malicious.
Just… misunderstood.

And when she said it, something in me whispered,
"I know that feeling."

Because if I'm being honest with you, sis?
I've felt misunderstood for most of my life.

Not because I was trying to be difficult, loud, sharp, or "too much."
But because I was wired differently than the rooms I was placed in.

Growing Up in the Inner City

Growing up in the inner city, you're surrounded by people who talk like you, walk like you, dream like you, and survive like you. You don't feel different. You don't feel out of place. You feel normal. Because the environment matches your wiring.

But the moment you step outside of that world?
Everything changes.

I remember stepping into corporate for the first time — a world where people spoke differently, moved differently, and carried themselves with a confidence I wasn't taught.

I walked in with the language of my community. Broken English wasn't broken to me — it was culture. Identity. Home. But corporate didn't see culture. They saw "incorrect."

I'll never forget the day I said the "bulp" wasn't working — the way we naturally pronounced it in my community. And in front of the entire office, the HR manager stopped me and slowly said:

"Say b-u-l-b."

SIS, YOU'RE NOT DIFFICULT, YOU'RE MISUNDERSTOOD

Loud.
Corrective.
Public.

I swallowed my embarrassment like it was part of the air.
Policies were soon introduced stating that only proper English should
be spoken at work — because of me.

It felt like my identity was being peeled off my skin. Piece by piece. I
didn't like it. I felt like I was constantly on eggshells.

But as time went on, I practiced. I learned. I grew. And I became grateful for the growth. I became grateful for her efforts to steer me in the
right direction.

Except… growth has consequences too.

Because the moment I went back home speaking proper English —
the same people I loved started whispering:

"You're acting like you're better than us."
"You forgot where you come from."
"You think you're brand new."

Sis, do you know what it does to your confidence when the room you
outgrew calls you disloyal…
…and the room you're growing into calls you unprepared?

You're too much for one world.
Not enough for the other.

That alone can break a woman.

But as time went on, I learned something powerful:

You cannot live your life trying to satisfy two worlds that never agreed on who you should be. You will drive yourself crazy **trying to meet expectations that were never aligned in the first place.**

And while I used to fight so hard to fit in, I had to accept that I'm different. Built differently, raised differently, and experienced differently. Life will look different for me in every room I enter because of that. And that's OK.

I've been in spaces where the pace didn't match my mind.
Where warmth was prioritized before clarity.
Where connection came before execution.
Where moving fast felt like moving "wrong."
Where having vision didn't feel like a gift — it felt like something I had to tuck away just to function or to be chosen.

I worked hard.
I gave my whole heart.
I showed initiative.
I solved problems early.
I brought excellence — the way my brain is wired to do.

But one small detail… one simple oversight… suddenly felt bigger than all the brilliance I carried.

Not because I wasn't capable.
Not because I wasn't enough.
But because my mind moves quickly, and sometimes that speed means I miss something someone else needed. And suddenly, I don't belong in those spaces. Suddenly, everything I was capable of gets pushed to the back burner. There are going to be times when you make a mistake, like me? I always took accountability — gracefully — but sometimes it didn't stop me from questioning myself.

SIS, YOU'RE NOT DIFFICULT, YOU'RE MISUNDERSTOOD

What am I doing wrong?
Why wasn't I chosen?

But by asking those questions, I realized:

The problem wasn't the environment.
The problem was that I would always try to shrink myself to fit into it.

Sis, pain enters the picture the moment you silence the strengths God placed in you.

I wasn't misunderstood because the people were wrong —
I was misunderstood because I was trying to bury my own gifts to blend in.

The Truth I Had to Learn

Some environments will misread your strength as a flaw.
But the right ones will see you for who you are.

That doesn't mean you ignore your blind spots.
That doesn't mean you stop growing.
Maturity requires you to strengthen your weaknesses.

But here's the balance:

Do your work.
Grow where you need to grow.
And if after all that, you STILL cannot thrive there…
it's simply not your space.

And when you recognize that, go on and be **EXTRAordinary**. Build your own room, create it with as many windows and doors as **you need.** When that time comes, don't you dare think less of yourself.

It's not a judgment.
It's not arrogance.
It's not you thinking you're better.

It's alignment.

Some things just aren't yours — and that is okay.

What God Says About Your Wiring

It took me quitting the war I was fighting with myself and leaning into who God made me to be, and that's when this scripture finally made sense:

"I praise You because I am fearfully and wonderfully made." — **Psalm 139:14**

Fearfully. Wonderfully. Intentionally.

God doesn't make mistakes.
He didn't miswire you.
He didn't misplace you.
He didn't give you a fast mind, strong voice, or visionary spirit by accident.

You are designed on purpose for a purpose.
If the door keeps closing, that's because God has bigger plans in store for you — **or maybe the timing simply isn't right yet.** Sometimes,

being misunderstood is God's gentle nudge that you're trying to belong in a place He never assigned you.

Sis, Own Your Make-Up

You were not made to fit into every room.
You were made to bring light to the rooms that align with your calling.
Be the light and the salt of every room you enter.

Stop dimming yourself for comfort.
Stop apologizing for evolving.
Stop shrinking to avoid judgment.
Stop fighting the very wiring God placed inside you.

You are HER.

Bold. Brilliant. Becoming.

And you are worthy of spaces that see you clearly.

Now that you understand your wiring — your identity, your evolution, and the truth about why you were misunderstood — it's time to talk about what comes next: **protecting the woman you're becoming.** Because once you stop shrinking, once you stop apologizing, once you stop bending yourself into the shape other people prefer... you must create boundaries that honor your growth. Confidence is who you are. Boundaries are how you protect her.

Let's talk about it, sis.

HER Mirror Moment: Sis, Say It Out Loud

"I no longer shrink to fit environments not
designed for me.
I honor my growth, my wiring, my evolution,
and my becoming.
I am not misunderstood — I am becoming **HER**."

HER Word: Sis, Let's Reflect

Before we move on, grab your *"Her Reflection"* journal. These
questions are here to help you see how powerful you

Your Reflection Questions

1. When have you felt caught between two worlds?
2. Where have you felt "too much" for one group and "not
   enough" for another?
3. What parts of yourself did you silence to fit in?
4. Who are the people who truly see you — without needing
   translation?

8

SIS, LET'S TALK BOUNDARIES

"Every time I set a boundary, I'm not pushing people away,
I'm pulling myself closer to peace."

— *Yanique P. Walters*

I n the previous chapter, we spoke about confidence, but confidence also means knowing how to set boundaries without apology. I know this is one of the hardest things for women to do. Many of us believe that setting boundaries will cause a man to leave. Others worry it will push away friends or family who think we're being too difficult. But Sis, let me ask you this: would you rather stay uncomfortable just to keep the peace, or finally honor your needs and stand in your truth?

Let's talk about what it really means to set boundaries.

SIS, YOU ARE HER

Setting boundaries means clearly communicating your limits, both physically and emotionally. It's about making your needs and expectations known and confidently stating what you will and will not accept. Boundaries aren't about building walls; they're about building self-respect.

The truth is, many of us internalize our boundaries and expect people to "just know." We assume they'll magically avoid crossing our lines. But Sis, people are not mind readers. Waiting for someone to hurt you just so you can react only leads to more pain and misunderstanding. Instead, let's try to be clear. Be firm. Be vocal.

Setting boundaries shows self-awareness. It shows that you understand your values and what you're comfortable with. Without boundaries, we become easy to manipulate.

Just look at Cassie's situation. Her entire existence was centered on pleasing P. Diddy. She didn't feel safe or empowered enough to say no. She didn't set boundaries, and it cost her.

Now, let's be real: setting boundaries can feel challenging. Whether it's telling your boss you can't take on another last-minute assignment or telling your partner you're not comfortable with something, it's tough. But it's necessary. If you don't protect your peace, no one else will.

And listen…, don't just set the boundaries, that's not enough. You have to enforce them. If you tell your friends you'll attend the party as long as there's no smoking around you, and they light up anyway, you have every right to leave. That's not being extra, that's honoring yourself.

I want you to also know that just because you haven't verbalized your boundaries doesn't mean others don't recognize they exist. Sis, they might be respecting a boundary you never meant to set.

I recently had an encounter with my family that really made me sit with myself and reflect.

I was going through a rough patch. I was visibly struggling, and anyone with two eyes could see it. But nobody offered to help. Not a check-in, not a "you need anything?" Nothing. And because I'm naturally used to handling things on my own, I kept pushing through. In my mind, whether they helped or not, it had to get done regardless. I was in survival mode. But if I'm being honest, deep down I was side-eyeing the whole situation like, "I can't believe they're really just watching me do all this alone. This is ludicrous."

Meanwhile, they were apparently looking at me and saying, "Wow, she's handling it all on her own."

When I finally brought it up, their response was, "You never asked."

That stung a little, but they weren't wrong. I didn't ask.

As much as a part of me felt like I *shouldn't have to*, the other part had to admit that I never communicated what I needed. As a result, they thought they were respecting my space. Respecting my independence. Respecting what they thought was a boundary I had set.

Whew!

That moment taught me something important: Sometimes people aren't neglecting you, they're only honoring the boundary you never meant to set. And the truth is, it's okay to ask for help. And it's also okay to say,

"I've got this." The key is just to be clear either way. You can't expect people to read your silence as a cry for support.

My takeaway? Set the boundary *and* the expectation. Don't assume people should just know.

Why Boundaries Matter

As you can see above, I haven't always been good at setting boundaries. I've struggled with jobs, relationships, friendships, and even with family. I stayed silent because I didn't want the conflict, or I was scared. Scared of losing love, support, or opportunities. But I eventually realized that fear was ruining my life.

Setting boundaries promotes self-respect. It tells the world, "I matter. My peace matters." It also reduces stress and anxiety. When you clearly know your limits and confidently speak up, you avoid burnout, resentment and being overwhelmed. Boundaries help protect your emotional and mental health.

Plus, they clarify expectations. People know what you will and won't tolerate. I once watched a couple's interview where the man shared how his now-wife became the one. He had been dating multiple women, and when she found out, she said, "I don't play games," and walked away. Weeks later, he realized five women didn't measure up to her. He came back, ready to commit. See, boundaries do set the tone early.

Examples of Setting Boundaries:

- Saying no to unreasonable requests

- Setting time limits for work and not checking emails after hours

- Communicating emotional needs clearly in relationships

- Respecting your physical space and making it known to others

Sometimes, we'd rather feel chosen than feel safe. But choosing to keep the peace by people-pleasing only robs you of your power.

Signs That You Lack Boundaries

Ask yourself:

- Do I feel guilty saying no?
- Do I often feel drained after interactions?
- Am I always overextending myself for others?

If you answered yes to these questions, then Sis, it's time to check your boundaries.

Boundaries vs. Ultimatums

It's important that we know the difference between boundaries and ultimatums because what I don't want you to be doing is controlling people. Boundaries are about protecting yourself. Ultimatums are about controlling someone else. There's a difference.

- **A boundary:** "If you raise your voice again, I'll Walk away from the conversation."
- **An ultimatum:** "If you ever yell at me again, we're done." See the difference? One comes from self-love, the other from control.

How to Start Setting Boundaries

- **Start small.** Practice saying no without over-explaining. Use "I" statements. I learned this a long time ago: use "I" statements, "I feel disrespected when…" not "You're disrespecting me." Because you don't want to be passing the blame onto the person. They may feel attacked and become defensive.

- **Write your boundaries down.** Rehearse them. That way, when the time comes to speak up, it won't feel so foreign.

- **And yes, enforcing boundaries might cost you people.** Sis, it'll help you find yourself. It'll help you not to lose yourself.

Boundaries in Dating

This is where many of us slip. Let's fix that. Here are examples of dating boundaries:

- "I don't move in until we're married."
- "I won't be sexually intimate until I feel emotionally safe."
- "No social media posts until I'm comfortable."
- "No large purchases until we're married."
- "No kids until marriage."
- "I don't tolerate ghosting, gaslighting, or inconsistency."

You're not asking for too much, you're setting your standards.

Guilt-Free Goodbye

If someone keeps crossing your boundaries, you don't need closure. You need distance. You don't owe another explanation. Closure is a decision, not a discussion. Peace is better than being picked.

Remember, boundaries aren't about building distance. They're about building a life rooted in self-love and clarity. You don't need to tolerate behavior(s) that drains you just to keep someone around.

And when your boundaries are repeatedly disrespected? Walk away. Choose peace. Choose you.

Jesus often walked away from the crowd to rest. He didn't argue. He didn't explain. He just withdrew. You need to know when to do the same.

For the longest time, I was against blocking. I used to tell my friends, "Girl, I don't need to block, I'm great at ignoring." But here's what I've learned:

Even if I don't respond, the moment they reach out, my peace is disturbed. The energy is back in my space. The disrespect tries to seep through the cracks. I have since became a blocker.

I remember one guy in particular. I told him I wasn't interested anymore. And his response? "F**k you!" (Yeah… I bet he wanted to.) But I didn't block him fast enough because the moment he realized the outburst didn't shake me, he started texting, calling, trying to walk it back.

"You calmed down yet?"
"Let's move forward."

And that's when it clicked:
Oh, you don't respect me. You don't respect my "no". You're not reaching out to repair; you're reaching out to regain control.

SIS, YOU ARE HER

So, I blocked him.

And Sis? I haven't lost sleep since.

Protecting your peace isn't petty, it's necessary. If they won't honor your boundary, then remove their access to you.

Up next, we're diving into something just as important: believing you're worthy of real love. Because Sis, you are not hard to love, you're just asking the wrong people to love you.

HER Mirror Moment: Sis, Say It Out Loud

"I am allowed to say no.
I am allowed to protect my energy.
I am not too much; I'm just finally enough for myself."

HER Words: Sis, Let's Reflect

Sis, you've made it through another powerful chapter, and I want you to pause for a moment. This wasn't just about setting rules, it was about protecting your peace, your heart, and your future.

Now let's grab your journal, yes, the one you said you were going to buy from chapter 1, your "HER Reflection journal" and get into it. These questions aren't for me. They're for you. Answer them honestly. No filters. No pretending. Just you and your truth.

Your Reflection Questions

1. Where in your life have you allowed people to cross lines that you never actually gave them permission to cross?

2. What's one boundary you know you need to set, but have been afraid to?

3. How would your life feel if you honored your limits without guilt or apology?

4. Is there a part of you that still confuses love with overextending yourself?

9

SIS, YOU ARE NOT HARD TO LOVE

"I am not hard to love; I was just giving my softness to people who didn't know what to do with it."

— Yanique P. Walters

S is, I see those eyes widening. You're thinking, *Yass, this is my chapter!* But let's be real, you've been letting people get in your head, making you believe you're hard to love. Sis, no! We're not doing that.

A friend reached out to me recently, and she was really distraught. She said, "I'm tired of being needy. I just want to be like normal people. I love deeply and get attached too easily. Dating today is so difficult, I don't even know what to say to guys anymore." When I read her message, my heart broke a little.

We are living in the age of red-pill podcasts, TikTok opinions, and Instagram therapists, and let me not forget, the late Kevin Samuels. Everyone has something to say about dating, what to do, what not to do, where to eat, where not to go, how to act, what makes a woman high value, it's exhausting. I would be lying if I say I don't get why she, and maybe even you, would feel overwhelmed.

There was a time when I asked myself: Am I just difficult to love or be loved? Why can't I just shut up and bring peace like everyone says women should? Why do I always speak up, even when I know it may rock the boat? Why can't I just accept the lies if the man says he only lied because he didn't want to lose me?

But the more I thought about those questions, the clearer the answer became: I'm not the problem. And neither are you, well sometimes you are. But when you know deep down that you have done everything right and the outcome is not better, then it's fair to take a step back and look at the people you are attracting.

Let's be real though, the second guessing I was putting myself through, I know I am not the only one. But we are not doing that! You deserve to be with someone who doesn't lie in the first place. Someone who honors your presence enough to act right, not just clean up the mess after they've made you cry.

There are men out there that says "Do not swipe right unless you are healed. But let's be honest. Men who lead with that, usually need healing themselves.

Some of these men grew up in homes where love looked like survival. Where nobody asked how they felt.

SIS, YOU ARE HER

Where crying was ignored or punished.
Where vulnerability meant danger, not connection.

So, they learned to be:

- Strong.
- Quiet.
- Focused.
- Unbothered.
- Peaceful at all costs.

And yes, they will love you the best way they know how.
But their "best" might only stretch as far as **peace**, not **emotional presence**.

So when you cried,
or needed reassurance,
or wanted to talk through something...

They didn't know what to *do* with that.
Not because you were asking too much —
but because **no one ever held *their* hand, either.**

Their emotional development stopped at the moment they were forced to be strong.

And sis... you mistook that *silence* for maturity.
You thought his "calm" meant stable.
You thought his "unbothered" meant wise.
You thought his "I don't do drama" meant emotionally healthy.

But sometimes,
"I don't do drama" really means:
"I don't know how to handle emotional depth, so I rather shutdown than to deal with it"

And that's not love's fault.
And it's not yours.

Another area, I find is many of us try to change who we are to fit the mold that a man has created. This is not what we are doing either. If being yourself chases a man away, good. Let him run. That's one less heartbreak you have to nurse.

Love isn't supposed to hurt. It isn't supposed to feel like confusion or chaos. You should feel peace when you see his name pop up on your phone, not dread. I've been in relationships where seeing a man's name gave me anxiety because I never knew if he was calling with love or with attitude. I've also been with someone who made my heart skip in a good way. That kind of nervousness where you're excited to hear from him and not scared.

> *"The worst thing you can do is settle for a man who doesn't actually love you. No romance. No flowers. No surprises. No dates. No support. No reassurance. Just a man who shows up when he wants to be pleased and disappears when you need him."*
> **- Unknown**

I saw that quote somewhere and thought it was so real.

Sometimes, the men who hate you don't do it with fists, they do it with neglect. And while it's clear to outsiders when you've poured your everything into someone, it's hard to see the truth for yourself.

I remember dating a guy and sensing the shift. He started getting annoyed with everything I did. The way he looked at me felt cold, irritated, and over it. He didn't say it out loud, but his energy screamed it. And I? I didn't wait for the formal breakup. I left. Because if I'm not married to you, we don't have kids, and there's no shared mortgage or business, why should I be sitting around trying to make it work with your disrespect?

Don't get me wrong, we ought to fight if it's worth fighting for, but if it's pretty obvious there is no love, then leave.

Sometimes, people will provoke the life out of you for you to react so they can get their reason, when deep down they know they don't want to be there and nothing you did or did not do would have changed that. But they get the opportunity to paint you as the bad guy.

You are the writer of your story. The director of your life. If you're with someone who isn't right for your script, it's okay to change the scene or the actor. Rewrite the role. Walk away. You don't have to get attached just because he showed up. Attachment isn't love, its fear disguised as connection. And you are not desperate for oxygen. A man isn't air. You can breathe without him.

As long as you understand that finding love doesn't mean you should cling, you just need to connect. You'll no longer have to perform; because you know that you deserve to be seen.

Reframing Rejection

Sis, I know rejection hurts. I know it stings like bees and sometimes you just can't explain what you are feeling. But I challenge you to shift your mindset. View rejection as redirection. View it as God's way of protecting you from something you can't yet see. Maybe he wasn't meant to be your husband. Maybe he wasn't emotionally available. Maybe he wasn't sent for you. Let him go. Let me be clear, I am not telling you to give up on the man you are dating, I am asking you to fully assess the situation and view it for what it is. Nothing more, nothing less.

Loving Your Quirks, Your Softness, Your Depth

Part of becoming the woman you're meant to be is learning to love all of you, the loud laughs, the quiet thoughts, the deep love, the random quirks. You weren't made to blend in. You were made to be whole. And loving deeply? That's not a flaw. Sis, own that superpower.

Love Doesn't Require Performance

The right love won't ask you to shrink. The right person won't need you to hustle for worthiness. You won't need to be quiet just to be kept. Love isn't earned by walking on eggshells. Real love feels safe, soft, solid. You don't need to be perfect; you just need to be present.

You were never hard to love.

What you asked for wasn't "too much."
Your emotions weren't "dramatic."
Your needs weren't "a burden."
Your softness wasn't "weakness."

The problem wasn't you.

You were loving men who **did not have the emotional capacity to hold you. And those men don't deserve you!**

You just need someone who can hold you — not escape you.

SIS, YOU ARE HER

Someone who:

- Stays when emotions rise.
- Breathes instead of shutting down.
- Leans in instead of retreating.
- Sees your softness and knows it's sacred.
- Understands that love requires presence, not performance.

I remember trying to shrink my power because people told me it was too loud. You are so business like, so intimidating, so much. Be too much then!

No more shrinking.
No more silencing yourself to protect someone's comfort.
No more calling yourself "too much."

You were born to shine.

Somewhere along the way, someone mishandled your heart and made you feel like love had to be earned, performed for, or chased. But that was never yours to carry. Real love sees you, accepts you, and stays consistent. You don't have to shrink to be chosen. You don't have to prove your worth just to be held. Let's move on to the next chapter, where we'll talk about the importance of loving you, first and always.

HER Mirror Moment: Sis, Say It Out Loud

"I am not hard to love. I am learning to love myself so fully that anything less will feel foreign. I am enough, exactly as I am."

HER Word: Sis, Let's Reflect

Take a moment right now and grab your *"Her Reflection"* journal. It's time to explore where that lie started and replace it with truth. Be honest. Be gentle with yourself. Let this be the moment you stop questioning your lovability and start reclaiming your wholeness.

Your Reflection Questions

1. Have you ever silenced or changed yourself to make someone love me?
2. In what ways have you allowed rejection to shape how you see yourself?
3. What would loving yourself, just as you are, look like in your day-to-day life?
4. Is there a part of you you've been hiding because you thought it made you "too much" to be loved?

10

SIS, LET'S TALK SELF-LOVE AND SELF-CARE

"As you grow older, you will discover that you have two hands, one for helping yourself, the other for helping others."

— *Maya Angelo*

B uckle up, Sis, we're about to take off. Have you ever noticed what they say on an airplane before takeoff? "In the event of an emergency, place your oxygen mask on yourself first before assisting others." Now pause for a second and really let that sink in. Even in a crisis, they tell you to take care of you first. Not because it's selfish, but because it's necessary. You can't save anyone if you're gasping for air. You can't pour from an empty cup. And you definitely can't love someone else fully if you're not loving yourself first. Our love for others ought to be an overflow of how well we love ourselves.

That's what this chapter is about. This is your oxygen mask. This is your permission to stop putting everyone else first and leaving yourself for last.

Self-love and self-care are two of the hardest things for us women, especially mothers. We find time for everyone else and everything else. By the time we're done pouring into our kids, partners, jobs, friends, and family… there's nothing left for us. We're running on empty, smiling on autopilot, and calling it strength. I am a strong woman! Super Mommy! Nah girl, we have to find a way to prioritize us.

I can say "we", because I'm speaking from experience. My mornings start with my son on my mind, what he's going to eat, wear, how to get him out the door. Then I'm rushing to work, trying to stay on top of a hundred other things. It's a lot. Sometimes I am overwhelmed, and I know I'm not alone on this table.

We lose ourselves, gain weight, skip self-care, and then wonder why it feels so hard to bounce back.

That's why it's important to carve out time just for you. Even if it's only 15 minutes a day, make that time sacred. I make it a priority to:

- Move my body every day
- Drink my water
- Take care of my skin (yes, sunscreen is a MUST!)
- Eat what nourishes me, not what numbs me
- Mind my business

That Soca song, *drink water and mind my business*! Now I feel like dancing but let me get back to it.

Sis, these little acts of love? They add up. But what does self-love and self-care really mean?

What Self-Love Really Means

Self-love isn't just bubble baths and spa days. It's choosing yourself. It's honoring your needs. It's looking in the mirror and speaking kindly to the woman you see. Do not be like my old self. I was so hard on myself, I truly believed I was overweight, when I was nowhere close. That's how warped my view of myself had become.

It's also about setting boundaries, walking away from what hurts, and celebrating your wins, big or small.

Self-love says: "I matter." Not just when you're performing, achieving, or giving. Always. I hope this is something your parents instilled in you because that's needed.

What Self-Care Really Means

Self-care is any intentional action you take to care for your mental, emotional, and physical well-being. It's not selfish, it's essential. It's saying, "I matter enough to pause, breathe, and care for myself." Whether it's setting boundaries, drinking more water, or finally getting that check-up, self-care is how you protect your peace and conserve your energy so you can show up fully, in life and in love.

Why It's So Hard for Women (Especially Mothers)

We've been raised to believe our worth is in how much we give. If we don't give and let others feel good, then somehow, we are a bad person.

We're praised for being selfless to the point of exhaustion. But Sis, stress and tiredness is not love. Self-neglect is not a badge of honor. You deserve to be poured into as much as you pour into others.

"I saw a meme where a dad told his family that the first person to make a mess will be going to bed and the mom took up a box of toys, spilled it in the living room and said, "Well, it seems I'm going to bed now". That shows she is tired and was happy to find a reason to leave."

I know as moms, we carry guilt when we put ourselves first. But how can you raise a confident child if you're constantly teaching them that Mommy doesn't matter? Doesn't sound logical, right? And if you are raising girls, your daughters need to see how Mommy loves on herself, too.

Simple Daily Self-Care Practices

I am sharing these practices that I do on a daily basis with you, but you can find what works for you—as long as you are taking time to care for yourself.

- Wake up 15 minutes earlier to stretch and pray
- Drink water mixed with apple cider vinegar and lime before coffee
- Shower and put on your morning facial routine (sunscreen is a must)
- Put on something that makes you feel good (even if it's just a pair of earrings)
- Affirm yourself every morning
- Practice breath work or a 5-minute meditation
- Go outside for fresh air and sunlight

Self-care doesn't have to be complicated. It just has to be consistent.

Loving Your Body While You Heal

Your body has carried you through heartbreak(s), long nights, busy days, and countless emotional battles. It deserves love, not punishment.

Talk to your body the way you'd talk to your best friend:

- "Thank you for getting me through today."

- "You're still beautiful, even in transition."

Feed her well, keep her moving and compliment her. Even when you don't feel good about yourself at that moment. Your body is not the enemy

Consistency is the key but don't let the fact that you don't think you will remain consistent prevent you from starting in the first place. Just do it when you can.

Learning to Accept Compliments

Hey beautiful, you look amazing today!

Yes you, why are you looking behind?

I notice that many women love to deflect compliments like they're grenades. Someone says, "You look beautiful," and we say, "Oh, it's just the filter," or "I look a mess!" I used to be notorious for saying, "Oh, it's getting old now—it's an old dress." Oh, my hair, I did this 3 weeks ago.

Sis, stop it!

Say, "Thank you." Let it land. Because *every time you reject a compliment, you're reinforcing the lie that you're not enough.* And you are!

Detaching from External Validation

Likes, follows, and comments are not the measure of your worth. Neither is the attention you get (or don't get) from men or even women, cause a lot of us are in competition with the women online. If your confidence only shows up when you're praised, then it's not rooted. If it's taken away, then who do you become? Sad? Depressed?

Let your validation come from within. Be proud of the way you've kept going. You don't need anyone to clap for you if deep down inside you feel that you have accomplished something that you set out to. Let your confidence be the loudest thing in the room—even if no one claps.

I am not fully done with you on loving on yourself, so I'll circle back in the next chapter to remind you to update those damn photos and stop overusing them filters. You are beautiful, believe that!

HER Mirror Moment: Sis, Say It Out Loud

"I am worthy of my own love, time, and attention. I am choosing to show up for myself every day."

HER Word - Time to Reflect

Now Sis, grab your *"Her Reflection"* journal and take a few minutes to reflect. This moment is for YOU. How you can carve out time for yourself. If you have the journal, there will be a worksheet to fill out.

Your Reflection Questions:

1. What does self-love look like in your life right now?
2. What daily habit(s) can you add or change to care for yourself better?
3. In what ways have you tied your worth to how much you do for others?
4. Where in your life are you settling for survival instead of choosing softness, joy, and rest?

11

SIS, UPDATE THOSE PHOTOS

"I don't need to shrink, edit, or filter myself to be loved. The right one will recognize me—exactly as I am, not as I was."

— Yanique P. Walters

Sis, can we have a heart-to-heart real quick? It's time to update those photos.

Why are you still leading with a version of yourself that doesn't even exist anymore? Maybe you've gotten older. Maybe your body's changed. Maybe you've healed, grown, evolved, and that's a blessing. But your dating profile is still giving 2017 vibes. Heavily filtered. Angled to the gods. Sis, come on now… stop playing.

Let's be real, people are noticing, heck, men are noticing.
They're showing up, expecting one woman but meeting someone completely different. And it's not even about looking "better" or

"worse", it's about **truth**. It's about being seen for who you are **right now,** not a perfectly curated, touched-up version of who you used to be.

You don't have to catfish anyone to feel worthy of love. The real you is more than enough.

I watch *Catfish* sometimes and yeah, I laugh, but whew, some of those episodes hit differently now. Because most of those stories? They're rooted in **insecurity**. And I get it. When your confidence is low, it's easier to hide behind good lighting and old angles than it is to risk being rejected for the real you.

But Sis… if we're on this journey of healing and self-worth, it starts with **showing up.** Not as who you were 20 pounds ago. Not as who you think they want. But as **you**, the version of you that's standing tall today.

Let me tell you a little story. One of my girls finally updated her profile after years of recycling the same old pics. She was terrified, convinced she wouldn't get a single swipe. But girl… she started having better conversations, better connections, and one guy even told her, "You look confident, and that's what caught my eye."

It wasn't the outfit or the angle.
It was her truth.

So why do we hold onto old photos so tightly? Because sometimes, they remind us of when we felt most beautiful… most desired… most enough. But Sis, **you are not frozen in time.** You are evolving. You are still beautiful. Still worthy. Still Her.

Confidence isn't about being the youngest or the slimmest. It's about being secure in the woman you are **right now**.

And listen, I'm not saying you can't throw on a filter or edit your lighting. I do it too sometimes, to brighten a photo or make the background pop. But what I don't want is to look back and not recognize the woman I presented to the world. I don't want to be seen as fake. I don't want to catfish. I want to be **me**.

Need a quick profile refresh? Try this:

- Snap 3 fresh photos that reflect how you actually look right now.
- Use natural lighting and let your personality shine. Smile, laugh, be you!
- Skip the filters. Let them see your glow, not your blur. Let the sun kiss you!
- Rewrite your bio to reflect the woman you are today, not the girl you used to be.

Showing up honestly is a form of **self-love**. It says, *"I trust that the right one will love me exactly as I am."* That's powerful. That's freeing. Because when you stop hiding, you start healing.

No more overthinking. It's either they like you or they don't and if they don't? That's none of your business.

This doesn't mean you can't show up as your best self. Do your hair. Beat your face. Throw on that outfit that makes you feel like **that girl**. Just make sure it's **you**, not a pixelated version of someone you think you have to be to be loved. Not those AI curated images.

Sis, the right one will want **you**. The you that's healing, glowing, and growing. So go ahead, take new photos. Show up. Upload with confidence. Don't get carried away by the number of reactions or comments. And if you're feeling bold, tag me. Let me hype you up.

Because you don't need to pretend to be worthy of love, you already are. Take it from someone who used to hide at some point.

The Photo Healing Exercise: Reclaim the Girl in the Photo

Now that we've talked about showing up as your real self, let's go deeper.

Step One: Find *that* photo.
You know the one. Maybe you were smiling through survival. Maybe you were in love with someone who broke your spirit. Or maybe it was just a version of you that you thought people wanted. Sit with it. Don't scroll past it. Just breathe. Let it all come up.

Step Two: Write to her.
Talk to that version of you. Be honest but be gentle. Start with something like:

> *"Hey girl… I see you. Back then, you were…"*

Tell her what she didn't deserve. Tell her what you're proud of her for. Tell her what you know now that she couldn't see back then. Thank her for surviving.

Step Three: Rewrite the caption.
Look at what you originally wrote (if anything). Then write a new one. Give it a voice that reflects who you are now.
Old Caption:
New Caption:
Need a start? Try: *"She didn't know her worth yet, but she was never less worthy."*

Step Four (optional): Recreate the photo.
Same pose. Same vibe. Same girl, but now wiser, grounded, and glowing. Put both photos side by side and remind yourself:
I'm still her. Just evolved.

Let this be your mirror moment. Not a moment of shame, but of celebration.
You're not broken.
You're becoming.

In the next chapter, we're shifting gears to talk about what abuse really looks like, because if you're healing, you have to protect yourself from anything that could set you back physically, mentally, or emotionally.

HER Mirror Moment: Sis, Say It Out Loud

"I am proud of who I am today. I release the need to hide and trust that I am lovable just as I am."

HER Word – Sis, lets reflect

Now Sis, go grab your *"Her Reflection"* journal, the one that goes with this book. Flip to the chapter with these questions, and let's go! Keep healing, keep growing, and keep showing up — fully and fearlessly. Because you, Sis, are more than enough.

Your Reflection Questions

1. What are you afraid people will think if they see the real you?
2. What part of yourself have you been hiding, and why?
3. What would it look like to show up authentically in your next dating profile or relationship?
4. What outdated image of yourself are you still holding onto, and how is it keeping you small?

SIS, HERE'S THE TRUTH I HAD TO LEARN

Sis, these are the things I wish I knew that I want you to take away from PART 2.

Chapter 6: Sis, Let's Talk Confidence

- Confidence isn't something you either have or don't, it's something you build, moment by moment.
- The loudest person in the room isn't always the most confident, true confidence is quiet, rooted, and unshakable.
- You can be the most beautiful woman in the room and still not feel worthy if your inner voice is cruel.
- Confidence doesn't mean you never feel doubt, it means you move anyway, even with shaky knees.
- A confident woman isn't arrogant, she's simply tired of begging for permission to exist fully.

Chapter 7: Sis, You're not Difficult, you're Misunderstood.

- Evolving doesn't make you better than others — it makes you better than who you used to be.
- You will always feel misunderstood in rooms that were never built for your wiring.
- Some people only loved the version of you that stayed small.
- You don't need to shrink to be loved. You don't need to tone it down to be accepted. Your power is not a liability, it's a gift.
- You don't owe anyone an apology for becoming the woman God intended you to be.

Chapter 8: Sis, Let's Talk Boundaries

- A boundary is not a punishment; it's a declaration of self-respect.
- If someone gets upset because you set a boundary, that's the exact reason you needed it.
- Boundaries aren't just for others; they're a way to love and protect yourself.
- The people who love you will learn to respect your "no."
- Setting a boundary isn't rejection, it's redirection toward alignment.
- Peace feels lonely at first when you're used to chaos, but it's worth every ounce of discomfort.

Chapter 9: Sis, You Are Not Hard to Love

- Needing love deeply doesn't make you weak, it means your heart still works.
- The right love won't confuse you. It won't make you beg, chase, or break yourself to fit in.
- Rejection doesn't mean you're unworthy, it just means that person wasn't capable of loving you right.
- You don't have to shrink yourself to be kept. You were never meant to be small.
- Real love will honor your softness, not punish you for it. You are not asking for too much. You're just asking the wrong person.
- Attachment is not love. And fear is not connection.
- You are not hard to love. You've just been in places that didn't know how to receive your kind of love.

Chapter 10: Sis, Self-Love and Self-Care

- Self-love is not selfish; it's your soul's survival plan.
- You don't have to earn rest. You don't have to prove your worth through exhaustion.
- When you stop abandoning yourself, everything starts to shift.
- If you're waiting until things calm down to care for yourself, you'll always be waiting.
- You can't teach your children self-worth if you don't model it.
- Self-care doesn't need to be aesthetic; it just needs to be consistent.

Chapter 11: Sis, Update Those Photos

- You don't have to hide the woman you are now to be loved.
- Confidence looks better than any filter you could ever apply.
- The right person will recognize your glow without needing you to edit it.
- The version of you from five years ago isn't better, she's just different.
- You're not being vain by showing up fully. You're being honest.
- Letting go of old photos is symbolic; it's choosing to stop clinging to a version of yourself that you've already outgrown.

PART THREE

Sis, Let's Call It What It Is.

Not every "love" is real. Here's where we unlearn the pain.

12

SIS, THAT'S NOT LOVE – THAT'S ABUSE

"Love doesn't bruise. If it leaves you questioning your worth, isolating your voice, or fearing for your peace, it's not love."

— *Yanique P. Walters*

I f there's one thing many of us have learned the hard way, it's this: sometimes we will hold onto someone even when it's hurting us. We convince ourselves that the pain is worth it, that love requires sacrifice, that if we just love harder, they'll finally choose us, respect us, or stay.

But love should not require you to shrink, silence yourself, or abandon your own heart. That isn't love, Sis. That's harm. And that's why this chapter matters.

SIS, YOU ARE HER

We need to talk about what abuse really is because sometimes, it's not just the slap, the scream, or the bruise. Sometimes, it's the silence. The control. The guilt trips. The fear.

I grew up hearing twisted ideas of love: "If he didn't love me, he wouldn't hit me." Sis, do you really believe the lies they told us when we were little? Love is not supposed to hurt or leave you confused. A person who loves you will never want to harm you in any way. I witnessed abuse in my own community. I saw women cry behind closed doors and cover their bruises with shame and makeup. I once tried to step in, and I was told to "stay in a child's place." That left me confused me as a child. I couldn't understand why it was okay for someone to be hurt in the name of love. But as an adult I understand clearly that love never harms.

But instead of taking that on as my definition of love, I made a vow to myself from a young age: the moment I see any sign of abuse, I'm gone. I even told one of my exes plainly, "If I ever see any form of abuse, that's it for me," because I could see him struggling to control his anger.

A few weeks later, he confirmed my fears — and that was my sign to leave for good. It wasn't just bottled emotions; it was his nature. A person's true character can only stay hidden for so long. That's why you must be sensitive enough to recognize every red flag — they always show up during the dating season.

And guess what? That was the end of that relationship. Because I'm not going to tolerate any form of abuse, not then, not now, not ever.

Sis, I did see the red flags early, and instead of leaving, I decided to give a warning. Well, look where that warning got me. The reality is, what you allow is what continues. When someone realizes they can get away with hurting you, they often don't stop.

And not all abuse leaves bruises. Emotional abuse cuts deep. Words stick. Manipulation lingers. And sometimes, the pain we can't see is the pain that breaks us the most.

One of my friends was isolated by her partner. He slowly cut her off from friends and family. It was control, disguised as care. It wasn't love; it was ownership. Abuse thrives in silence and secrecy. If he can isolate you, then he has all the power.

Girl, you are not a beating stick. You are not someone's emotional punching bag. You are worthy of love, care, peace, and protection. I want you to be able to recognize when you are in an abusive situation, so let's break this down.

Red flags aren't silent. They speak. They scream. They burn. They sting. They are as red as coal, emitting heat and tension. As red as pepper, stinging the eyes and leaving discomfort that words cannot fully explain. As red as open wounds that never heal when you keep dressing them up with excuses. They are there, flashing, waving, yelling, begging you not to ignore them. Love is not meant to be tolerated in pain. It is not a battlefield for proving how long you can endure before breaking. When you see the signs, listen.

And when you see green flags, don't be too scared to believe them. Green flags are like trees. They may start small, but when watered with consistency, they blossom. They stretch out in grace. They multiply. They give shade and shelter. They bring fresh air and relief. A healthy love grows like that. It refreshes you, not depletes you. It does not seek to change your essence but creates a safe space for your roots to deepen and your leaves to flourish. Pay attention to the growth that peace brings. Love is meant to feel like that, like coming home, not like surviving a war zone.

We love to call it "just ups and downs." We excuse it with, *"He's trying."* But sis… at some point, you have to ask: *what am I trying to hold on to?*

We'll go deeper into the topic of red flags in Chapter 15, "Sis, Red Flags Aren't Decorations."

Rada Darling, the wife of Michael Blackson, a popular comedian, was in the blogs and she opened up and said the words too many women are afraid to say out loud:

> *"While I thought I had all the support in the world, I find myself walking alone depending on my little man."*

She hid behind her smile. She admitted postpartum was rough. And instead of comfort, her words sparked public backlash, followed by **Michael Blackson's clapback**, reminding her:

> *"It's not wise to talk sheet (I think he meant shit) about the hands that feed you."*

That line? That's where a lot of women lose their voice. Because it's hard to speak up when the one you depend on is also the one who can use that power against you.

Michael later said he misunderstood the post, claiming it wasn't about him, and that he tours often but supports her in other ways. That may be true. But what many of us saw, what too many women recognize, is the **emotional gap that forms when you're doing life with someone**

but still feel alone. And that's not partnership. That's not love. That's survival… in silence.

Let's Be Real, Sis

Some women stay because of the lifestyle.
Some stay because "he's not all bad."
Some stay because they've invested too much to walk away.
But here's the truth: **It will always feel like too much to leave if you've never positioned yourself to stand on your own.**

I remember the day my ex, the one I lived with, said to me, *"Go get your own f**ing place."**
And you know what I did?
I bought a house and left.

Why? Because I **refuse** to let a man have that kind of power over me. That's not being masculine. That's being wise. And I know it's not easy for everyone to up and do that because buying a house isn't small fry. But the point is to ensure that you position yourself in a way that you are not 100% dependent on another person. Find a side hustle if you don't have a job. There are so many work from home opportunities these day.

Sis, Please Hear This:

- Find a hustle.
- Stack your money.
- Start the business.
- Learn the skill.
- Go to therapy.
- Build community.
- Stay soft but stay ready.

Don't wait until you're humiliated to remember your value. **Position yourself before you ever need rescuing.** Because when the love runs low, the lifestyle won't hold you.

Understanding the Cycle of Abuse

Abuse often follows a cycle:

1. **Tension Building:** You feel like you're walking on eggshells.
2. **Explosion:** Yelling, hitting, or emotional manipulation.
3. **Reconciliation:** Apologies, gifts, promises.
4. **Calm:** Things seem fine… until it starts all over again.

This cycle creates confusion and emotional dependency. Sis, it doesn't have to continue.

Cassie shared that she had to go through brain-resetting therapy to heal from her experience. The pain lingers. It makes you scared, untrusting, and guarded in future relationships. But healing starts with you. You can break the cycle.

Emotional Impact

When abuse hits, it hits hard and deep. It can shatter your self-worth and lead to:

- Low self-esteem
- Anxiety
- Depression
- Guilt and shame
- Feeling unworthy of love

The worst part? It chips away at you so slowly, you don't always see it happening.

I remember when my ex told me I thought I was "all that" because I had a master's degree, but to "wait until I take off my hair and makeup." That stuck with me. For years, I wouldn't let anyone see me in my natural state. I didn't believe other men when they said I was beautiful, because his words echoed louder.

When I conducted my survey, one man said:

> *"I'm a root cause analysis type of guy. The question is, 'What's the origin of the low confidence?' If it is derived within our time together, I'm invested in resolving it. But if it persists and stems from her ex's words—words that hold more weight than mine, then I'm out. This happens a lot. I've left women who were unable to move past an ex's voice."*

Sis, that was a wake-up call. We have to be careful what we carry into our next relationship, especially the lies someone else told us about ourselves.

Building a Support System

Sis, you don't have to go through this alone. Talk to someone. Reach out to a therapist or counselor. Call a domestic violence hotline. Join a support group, online or in person. Your pain deserves to be heard, and your healing deserves to be supported.

If you still feel love for the person who hurt you, don't shame yourself for that. Love doesn't just vanish because you walk away from abuse. When someone becomes both your safe place and your source of pain, your mind and body get wired to crave the very situation that's hurting you. The same hands that held you in comfort were the same hands that broke you, and your brain remembers the warmth just as much as it remembers the hurt. That's why you cling to the good moments, hoping they'll return, even if they come at a cost. Healing isn't about pretending you never loved them. It's about telling the truth; you did love them and still choosing yourself enough to walk away.

Steps to Leave Safely

If you're planning to leave:

- Create a safety plan
- Know where you'll go and who you can call
- Gather important documents and emergency funds
- Use code words with trusted friends
- Seek legal protection if needed

Your life matters. Your peace matters. You matter.

Reclaiming Your Power

I know it's hard to leave, especially when you love someone and have invested time and energy. I know starting over can feel exhausting in today's dating world. But leaving isn't weakness, it's bravery. It's choosing yourself even when you're scared. It's saying, "I deserve more than this."

Healing takes time, but it's possible. One step, one boundary, one affirmation, at a time.

Let this chapter be your reminder that:

- You are not broken

- You are not crazy
- You are not the cause of your abuse
- You are worthy of safety, peace, and unconditional love

And Sis… you don't have to wait until you're broken beyond repair. You can choose freedom. You can choose you.

Let's keep going. Your healing journey has only just begun. We will talk about what self-confidence is and how to reclaim it once you start losing it.

HER Mirror Moment: Sis, Say It Out Loud

"I am not hard to love. I am not broken. I am no one's punching bag. I deserve love that doesn't leave me bruised, physically, emotionally, or spiritually."

HER Word: Sis, Let's Reflect

Here comes the moment of truth. Open your *"Her Reflection"* journal and give your honesty a voice.

Your Reflection Questions

1. In what ways have you allowed emotional or verbal abuse to be normalized in your life?

2. Do you have a safety plan or support system in place if you were to ever feel unsafe in a relationship? If not, what steps can you take today to begin building one?

3. What fears or beliefs have kept you from leaving a relationship that is harming you?

4. How would your life change if you believed you truly deserved to feel safe, loved, and respected every day?

13

SIS, THAT MAN IS LOVE BOMBING YOU!

*"If he's falling in love before learning your middle name, that's
not romance, it's strategy. Real love takes time. And Sis, so
should you."*
— Yanique P. Walters

Have you ever met a man, and everything seems to be moving so fast? He's calling you "wifey" after a week, planning vacations, saying he's never met anyone like you… and meanwhile, you barely know his last name.

Hey, we all deserve good love. But Sis, let me caution you be mindful of those men who move at lightning speed to sweep you off your feet. Don't let your need for love override your discernment.

Because what feels like a fairytale today might have you crying at a bus stop tomorrow. (And yes, I said bus stop —you'll understand in a minute.)

A Real-Life Love Bombing Story
Let me tell you a story. Start the engine.

I met this man and for context on speed, let's put a month into perspective, January. When Valentine's Day rolled around, I got a surprise, roses delivered to my door with a note that read:

> *"Be my valentine, Yanique. Divine & Fine, unmatched, sophisticated, delightful & sweet—all the time. Makes me wish you were mine."*

Listen, I was single and not expecting anything, so that delivery? It gave me butterflies. But then, I paused.

How did he even get my address?
Turns out, he used little details I'd shared to look it up online. I won't explain how because I'm not giving anyone ideas, but let's just say that raised some red flags.

Still, I brushed it off as a sweet gesture from a man who was just really into me. We continued talking, and eventually, we went on a date. He said, "As long as you are with me, your money has no worth." Okurr, and let me tell you, he meant it. He paid for everything, down to a pack of gum. And it wasn't a cheap date.

Part of me was enjoying it. But another part? Side-eyeing the whole thing. I told him not to do anything that wasn't sustainable. His face shifted.

Then, toward the end of the time, he said something that froze me:
"What if I'm just love bombing the hell out of you, and I will soon drop you?"

Sir?!

I don't think he thought that one through. Anyone who knows me knows I analyze everything, and that line only confirmed what my intuition had already been whispering. Still, I played along, kept my guard up, and allowed things to reveal themselves. I already knew the situation was too ambiguous for me to start getting attached.

Then came the "I love you."

And I'm thinking, *what exactly do you love in just 3 months? My photos? My vibe? My passport stamps? What was it?*

I started asking questions and documenting everything. Because Sis, this wasn't just a man being romantic, this was a serial love bomber.

I say this because he also admitted women were still blowing up his phone, women he'd dated for two months or less, some he hadn't even slept with. What had them hooked? The plans he made with them. Promises of marriage, a future, everything they'd been dreaming of… then *poof.* He'd vanish!

One day, he sent me a video about "toxic dick" and said,
"I think I may have that. Why else would these women be obsessing over me?"

Whew. Let's pause.

What Is Love Bombing?

Love bombing is when someone uses intense affection, grand gestures, and over-the-top attention early in a relationship to hook you emotionally, before you've had time to process or assess whether it's real.

It looks like:

- Excessive compliments
- Saying "I love you" early
- Talking about marriage or moving in quickly
- Texting all day, needing constant communication
- Making you feel like you owe them commitment before it's earned

And here's the thing, Sis: real love can be sweet and thoughtful too, please don't go thinking that if a man is nice to you, then that means he is love bombing you. That's not what I am saying at all. But discernment is key. Don't be so love-blind that you miss the red flags waving in your face.

His "Bus Stop" Analogy

He told me he doesn't see it as love bombing, he just wants a relationship so badly that when he sees someone with potential, he goes all in.

He explained it like this:

> *"Imagine a man waiting at a bus stop, excited to go home. The bus arrives; he gets on, only to realize it's the wrong route. Now he must get off. But the bus driver was excited to have him on, enjoying the ride, confused why he's suddenly leaving."*

Sir, what?!

Let's be clear: the problem isn't missing a stop. It's getting on buses without checking the route first.

I asked him, "Am I the wrong bus too?" He said no. That he had "researched me" and I was the one. But Sis... his track record said otherwise.

His behavior wasn't about me; it was about him. The emotional high of pursuit, followed by the withdrawal when reality sets in. That's love bombing.

Sis, You're Not a Bus Stop

You are not a pit stop on someone's journey to self-discovery. You're the destination. You deserve someone who knows what route they're on before inviting you on the ride.

So, if you're uncertain, here are a few red flags to look for:

- He talks about forever before you've even had your first disagreement.
- You feel pressured to match his energy before you're ready.
- His vibe changes the moment you set a boundary.
- It feels overwhelming instead of steady and safe.

Protecting Your Heart

Here are a few steps you can take to protect your heart from these love bombers:

- Move at your pace
- Ask yourself: "Who is he when he's not trying to impress me?"
- Don't confuse intensity with intimacy
- Let time reveal the truth

- Boundaries are a filter, not a wall. They protect you

Sis, love bombing isn't about love, it's about control. It's about stirring up your emotions so quickly that you don't even have time to listen to your intuition. And let me tell you, your intuition is your superpower.

The minute something feels off, don't second-guess yourself. Pause and check. Don't let "potential" blind your judgment.

Real love won't confuse you. It won't come wrapped in chaos and dipped in anxiety. Real love will give you peace. Consistency. Clarity. Real love will let you breathe.

Spiritual Check-In

Proverbs 4:23 says, *"Above all else, guard your heart, for everything you do flows from it."*

God doesn't rush. God isn't in confusion or chaos. True love is rooted, not rushed.

The next time someone comes in hot, talking forever before you've even shared your favorite color, breathe. Take your time. Guard your heart. You're not being "difficult" for asking questions or slowing things down. You're being wise.

Remember This, Sis

You are the table. The blessing. The answered prayer. And any man who truly deserves your heart won't try to rush the process—he'll respect it.

In the next chapter, we will talk about these men who want you to be their mama. And no, we're not doing that either.

HER Mirror Moment: Sis, Say It Out Loud

"I am worthy of love that's real, not rushed. I protect my heart, honor my pace, and allow time to reveal the truth."

HER Word: Sis, Let's Reflect!

Listen, Sis. It feels amazing when a man drowns you in affection, gifts, and sweet words. But before you call it love, pause. Ask yourself: *is this genuine, or a performance?* These reflections aren't just for today, but for every season of your love life.

Your Reflection Questions

1. Have you ever been swept up in fast love that faded just as quickly?
2. What does healthy love look like to you now?
3. How can you slow things down when someone tries to rush intimacy?
4. Is there a part of you that confuses intensity with intimacy? If so, what has that cost you in the past?

14

SIS, HE'S NOT YOUR PROJECT

"I am not here to fix, prove, or beg. I'm here to be loved,
respected, and partnered with."
— Yanique P. Walters

My dad always told me, "Find a man who will love you and treat you right." And honestly? My dad did show me what love supposed to look like. Whenever I called, he showed up. Sometimes he showed up with an attitude, blaming my mom for always sending me to him, but he never let me go without. I felt protected.

My mom? Same mindset. She believed that if I had a man, he should be taking care of me. I remember being in college when she found out I had a boyfriend. Her immediate reaction? "Let him take care of you." I didn't fully understand what that meant back then, and to be honest, I'm still not sure I do now. But shout out to that man, he really did step up. He helped me stay on track in school. That's a story for another time, though. Let me not get sidetracked.

When Helping Becomes a Habit

Because of what I saw growing up, I naturally sought out men who were in a position to pour into me, the way I poured into others. And for a while, that worked. I attracted successful, established men. But eventually, I started questioning everything. I wondered if that was the problem all along. Maybe love wasn't about finding someone who had it all together. Maybe, I should just try the opposite. And I did.

I dated a man who had less than me. And whew... There was joy in that. I loved nurturing him, helping him get back on his feet. I felt needed. I thought to myself, maybe this is what real love looks like. Maybe if I give more, love will stay this time.

But over time, that became my pattern — seeking out men who needed saving. I convinced myself that if I helped them level up, they'd love me harder. Stay longer. Choose me forever.

The Reality Check

Sis... I was wrong.

And I know some of you know that sting, the heartbreak that comes when even the broke ones don't choose you. That's a different kind of low. I was out here pouring love into men who barely had a plan, promising loyalty and encouragement, and they still left. I heard things like, "I can't be with you right now. I'm not where I want to be," or "I feel less of a man because I can't provide for you."

I started thinking, Is it me? Is love ever going to find me? Maybe I'm too accomplished. Maybe I'm just too much.

But here's what I've come to understand. Sometimes, it's not about you at all. Sometimes, it's about him.

What the Survey Revealed

When I surveyed men for this book, one powerful insight kept showing up: The pressure to provide is real.

I asked, "Do you feel pressure to be a provider or to 'have it all together' before committing to a woman?" And here's how they responded:

- 43.5% said yes, very much—they feel enormous pressure to have their finances, emotions, and life in order before considering a serious relationship.
- 13% said sometimes — it depends on where they are in life.
- 26% said not really — they're more open to building together.
- 17.4% said no — they don't feel that pressure at all.

Even with varied answers, the message was clear: **Most men want to feel solid before showing up seriously.**

Whenever a man pulls away, it's not always a rejection of you. Sometimes it's his own inner voice saying, "You're not ready for her."

Sis, Stop Playing Savior

And if both the rich ones and the broke ones aren't choosing you, stop assuming you're the problem. Start seeing the truth: They didn't feel ready to love you the way you deserve.

When a man doesn't feel like a man, your presence feels like pressure. Your strength feels like a threat. Your success feels like a mirror he's not ready to face.

That's not your fault. That's not your burden. Pouring into a man who's leaking from wounds he won't even admit to is a full-time job. And when you already have a child, a career, and some healing to do… baby, that's too much.

Potential vs. Peace

I'm not saying don't stand by a man who's truly doing the work because not all men are like what I described above. But those who expect you to dim your light so they can feel tall? That's not it.

I once saw a meme that said:

- *"A man without peace will take yours."*
- *"A man without money will take yours."*
- *"A man without confidence will take yours."*

I felt that.

Nicknames and Red Flags

I once dated a man who had potential but couldn't see it in himself. He wasn't the tall, six-foot figure I imagined, but he made me feel seen. Still, his exact words were: "I'm not where I need to be to date you." He even nicknamed me "Big Money."

Let's pause for a moment: Ladies, can we stop romanticizing nicknames that are actually red flags? Because dating a man who isn't stable isn't just emotionally risky, it's spiritually draining. And no, this isn't about money or material things. It's about peace. Safety. Emotional security.

A Quick Bible Lesson: Leah's Story

Remember Leah? She married Jacob, but she was never his first choice. Jacob loved Rachel. And Leah? She was given to him by deception, and from the very beginning, she was trying to earn what Rachel already had effortlessly— his heart.

She gave Jacob's sons. Stayed loyal. Showed up. And every time she birthed a child, she said, "Now maybe my husband will love me." But it never changed anything.

Leah kept producing, hoping her love would be enough to be seen and chosen.

Love that you have to earn isn't love, it's performance. It's survival mode, wearing a lipstick

You Are the Prize

Sis, how many times have you done the same? Cooked. Cared. Waited. Helped. Prayed. Supported. Trying to prove that you were worth staying for?

You are not Leah. You do not have to hustle to be loved. You are not a placeholder. You are not a backup plan. You are not a reward for loyalty.

You are the prize, not a project. Stop fighting to be chosen by someone who was never sent to cherish you.

The Wake-Up Call

Sarah Jakes Roberts once said, "I'm not here to save anybody, I'm here to be loved, respected, and partnered with." That quote snapped me out of it.

I had to ask myself, what am I doing?

That's when it hit me: it's not about rich or poor, it's about values.

My New List

I then decided to sit down and made me a new list. What do I actually want in a relationship?

- Communication
- Loyalty
- Support
- Honesty
- Love
- Care

However, that package shows up, that's what I'm seeking.

Now it's your turn. Write down your non-negotiables. Not your mom's list. Not your friends'. **Yours!**

It should never be just about how much a man makes; it should be about how much he respects, values, and shows up for you.

Watch the Patterns

I used to think that if I dated a man who had less, he'd appreciate me more. That was my logic, until I heard Steve Harvey say: "A man shows love by what he does for you—not just what he says to you."

Whew. That was it.

I had been listening to promises, not watching patterns.

Sis, Evolve!

We live in a dating culture obsessed with the "3 sixes"—6 figures, 6 feet, 6 inches. And hey, I get it. We all want what we want. But sometimes I look around and think…no wonder we're in a dating crisis. Everyone's chasing the same prototype.

Sis, you are more than a relationship. You are purpose. You are presence. You are whole.

I still want a relationship. Of course I do. I can't wait for prince charming to find me. But until then? I'm not just waiting, I'm living. Traveling. Growing. Healing. Raising my son to be a man a woman would be proud to love. Becoming the woman, I would be proud to love.

You can do the same.

Stay Open, But Rooted

And no, I'm not saying close the door to love. I'm saying stay open to love but be rooted in you.

Join that gym. Start that hobby. Attend that conference. Go where the version of you you're becoming would go, and your partner may just meet you there.

Cameron Diaz took a long break from dating, worked on herself, then found deep love later in life with Benji Madden. You're not late. You're on time.

Let your journey lead you to someone who doesn't flinch at your power but falls in love with it.

Oprah said, *"The whole point of being alive is to evolve into the complete person you were intended to be."*

Sis… that's the mission. Until that person comes, trust your intuition and keep it pushing. Let's talk about your intuition next, cause some of us love to ignore it!

HER Mirror Moment: Sis, Say It Out Loud

"I am not a rehab center for broken men. I release the need to fix anyone. I deserve a love that's whole, not a job, disguised as a relationship."

HER Word: Sis, Let's Reflect!

It's journal time, Sis. Go ahead and grab your *"Her Reflection"* journal —it's time to check in with yourself. No fixing, no overthinking, no trying to be perfect. Just you, your pen, and some real talk on the page

Your Reflection Questions

1. Have you been choosing men based on their potential rather than their current values and consistency?
2. In what ways have you been trying to "fix" or "save" someone? And what did it cost you emotionally?
3. What are your non-negotiables in a relationship? Are you honoring those same values within yourself?
4. What values do you want in a partner, and are you giving those to yourself right now?

15

SIS, TRUST YOUR INTUITION

*"You don't need proof when God already gave you peace.
Trust the nudge. That's your spirit speaking."*
— Yanique P. Walters

How many times have you ignored that gut feeling — the one that pulls tight in your stomach or whispers quietly in the back of your mind? I have. More times than I'd like to admit. And I know I'm not alone.

God gave us intuition not to question it, but to trust it.

There were times I wasn't even close to a situation, yet I felt what was happening — and when I checked, I was spot-on. That's discernment. God's warning system wrapped in wisdom. And yet, as much as I had it, there were seasons when I silenced it.

I remember calling my ex one day. He said he was on the phone with his cousin and sent my call to voicemail. Under normal circumstances, that might have been fine… but I immediately felt that familiar stab, the one that whispered, "Nah, he's lying." My spirit felt unsettled. When I reached out again, I got his voicemail. I thought to myself, "nah, something isn't right."

As time passed, he called back and said he "just got out of the shower." But the math wasn't mathing nor was my spirit buying it. Lie after lie to cover the previous one and my intuition picked up on it each time. I'll spare you the details, but that night the truth came out — and my intuition had been right every step of the way.

That was the day I promised myself: **Never again will I doubt what I know in my spirit.**

But promises are easier said than kept.

When I Broke My Own Rule

Fast forward. I met a man who came on strong — texts, calls, consistency, conversations. He told me he was going through a divorce and even showed documents to prove it. I took him at his word.

I said to him, "Let's just get to know each other while everything finalizes." It felt responsible. Safe. Clear. Boundaries were being set. And I didn't see any harm in being friends at the time. He also reassured me that it would be done in 30 days because it's uncontested, I said cool.

But looking back, that was the first compromise. That was me cracking the door wide enough for deception to walk in — not because I intended to break my values, but because I trusted what he presented.

But as time went on, every action he took, something in my spirit wasn't settled.

Then came the inconsistencies:

- unexplained weekends
- odd behaviors
- two phones
- sudden distance

My spirit tugged, but I brushed it off, convincing myself I was overthinking. He's just busy. When really, I was ignoring the truth staring me in the face.

Then one night, everything came to light.

We were out late at night when his phone started ringing repeatedly. The number showed up under his daughter's name. But my intuition whispered, "This isn't right. Tell him to pick it up." That's how deceptive he was, saving the other woman's number under his child's contact.

Anyways, I encouraged him to answer — just in case it was an emergency.

The moment he picked up, a woman's voice came through the phone, hurt and furious:

"Where the hell are you? Why haven't you answered your phone?"

I asked him to put it on speaker. He did.

She immediately demanded, "Who is that?!"

He said, "That's Yanique, my girlfriend."

She screamed, **"How is she your girlfriend when I'm your girlfriend?"**

Sis… he froze. Heck, I froze. Reality froze. What did I just hear?

And here's the part that reveals just how deceptive he truly was:

It turns out he wasn't just lying to me. He had his wife, and also another woman who thought she was his future, planning to buy a house and create a life with him. Yep, the woman screaming on the phone wasn't even the wife.

Later, the **actual wife** contacted me and revealed that the divorce had already been dismissed, the very day after it was filed. And guess by who? Yup — the man himself. They were trying to work things out. He basically misled all of us. He was juggling **three women**, possibly more.

Sis, I thank God I wasn't deeply invested and was able to get out before emotional roots could grow. But even so, the real heartbreak wasn't him —it was realizing I had sensed the truth all along… and still silenced myself.

The Moment Everything Shifted

In the middle of the chaos, which went on for a few days, the other woman — the one who believed she was his future — said something to me that changed everything:

"I saw that you're a writer. You should write a book about this."

At first, I laughed. I thought it would make one heck of a drama piece —I've got enough to material to write a whole script about lies, deception, late-night calls and secret phones.

So I started writing just to get it out of my system. But as my fingers touched the keyboard, God spoke to me.

He said:
"That's not your purpose. While I don't agree with what you attempted to do, there are other women out there making the same mistake.
This isn't for drama.
This is for deliverance.
Women need your honesty.
They need your transparency.
They need your voice.
They need your warning."

"This is your opportunity to help, you need to turn your pain into purpose."

And just like that, the book you're holding was born — not from shame, but from purpose. Ideas started pouring out of me. Lessons I had learned, stories I had buried, topics women whisper about but rarely say out loud. I felt like I wasn't in control of my own fingers anymore. I was simply the vessel.

Owning My Part

Sis, this book was born from one of my lowest moments. Not to glorify the pain, but to show you that even your mess can become a message. I'm not here to pretend I made perfect decisions. I didn't.
In the moment, I was receptive of the connection — and I ignored the unease in my spirit.

But that choice doesn't define me. It revealed where I needed to grow. And that's the message I want you to take from this.

Sis, you're not the only woman who's ever made a decision that might have hurt someone else, especially when you were craving love or connection. Sometimes our desire to feel chosen can cloud the clarity God is trying to give us. That doesn't make you foolish or inherently selfish— it makes you human.

Growth begins when you can say:

"I see where I went wrong. Now I know better. Now I will do better."

That's wisdom. That's maturity. That's healing.

Sis, I share my story, but I know I am not the only woman who has ever been misled, deceived, or swept into something that didn't align with our values. You are not either. Please don't beat yourself up, life goes on.

You're not broken.
You're not weak.
You're not beyond restoration.

You're a woman who trusted too deeply, loved too honestly, and now has the wisdom to move differently.

Just remember, when dating, love isn't supposed to hurt. It's not supposed to leave you confused, anxious, or battling with other women for clarity. No man — single, married, separated, or otherwise — should be simultaneously damaging three women's **hearts**.

Trust what you feel the first time. Chances are, you are not wrong.

Intuition vs. Insecurity

I want to make it clear, that this chapter isn't about a man — it's about discernment. It's about intuition. The whispers. The nudges. The sick feeling in your stomach that tells you something isn't right, even when the words sound perfect.

Your intuition is NOT paranoia. Your intuition is divine. And the more you honor it, the more peace you protect.

- If your spirit feels uneasy, don't dismiss it.
- If a story sounds too polished, pause.
- If you're bending your boundaries to "keep the peace," slow down.
- If your peace disappears, something is wrong.

Quick Check: Is It Intuition or an Old Wound?

Because here's the truth, Sis:
You cannot trust your intuition if you haven't learned to tell your past pain from your present discernment.

Intuition is:
- calm but clear
- a steady knowing
- a quiet knowing, like the truth you can't un-know.

Insecurity is:
- loud and frantic
- anxious
- fueled by past hurt
- needing constant reassurance

Ask yourself: **"Is this a red flag... or an old wound?"**

Here are a few steps that you can take to reclaim your power if you find yourself in a similar situation:

1. **Block, delete, disconnect.** Silence isn't petty, it's necessary in those moments of chaos.
2. **Talk to someone you can trust.** Shame often dies in safe spaces.
3. **Focus on your healing.** Your next level requires your full attention.

Let This Be Your Wake-Up Call
You don't need to be someone's secret.
You don't need to compete.
You don't need to babysit brokenness.
You don't need to settle for intensity over intimacy.
You don't need to shrink your discernment to make someone comfortable.

Sis, you deserve love in the light.

You deserve clarity, consistency, peace, and truth.

But don't for a second think that because your intuition is talking to you, that you are crazy. You are NOT.
You are discerning.
And that is your superpower.

When you trust yourself more than you trust their words —
that's when everything shifts.

Next chapter, we're diving deeper into red flags — what they look like, what they don't look like, and how your intuition helps you recognize them early.

HER Mirror Moment: Sis, Say It Out Loud

"I deserve the truth. I am worthy of real love, not confusion. I will trust my discernment and protect my peace."

HER Word: Sis, Let's Reflect

Now Sis, lets grab your *"Her Reflection"* journal.

Before you move on, take a moment to sit with yourself. Reflect. Breathe. You don't need to justify what you know. You don't need anyone else to co-sign your spirit. This is about trusting you again

Your Reflection Questions

1. Have I ever ignored a gut feeling because I wanted someone to be right for me?
2. What patterns or red flags have I justified in the past, and why?
3. What does it look like for me to trust myself fully in love and relationships?
4. What would it feel like to live in full alignment with what I know deep down?

16

SIS, RED FLAGS AREN'T DECORATIONS

*"Red flags aren't red confetti, they're warnings dressed in
charm. Don't collect them. Walk away."*
— Yanique P. Walters

S is... last chapter was heavy, right?
Well, we've got a little more to talk about here. And this one?
It's about the red flags waving right in front of your face — the ones we pretend we don't see.

Because for many of us, red flags don't show up as bold banners.
They show up as sweet excuses.
As "He's just been through a lot."
As "Maybe I'm overreacting."
As butterflies that are really your intuition doing backflips trying to get your attention.

But let me say this plainly:

Red flags are not cute.
They're not quirks.
They're not personality traits you can fix.

They're warnings.
And we have to stop stitching them into blankets and wrapping ourselves in them just because we're scared to be cold.

Yes, Sis. I know. Those lonely nights?
They tempt you to settle.

And that old saying —
"The devil you know is better than the devil you don't."
That's not wisdom.
That's trauma talking.
That's fear talking.
That's someone who learned to normalize dysfunction and call it love.

But Sis, we're not doing that anymore.
Not every invitation to dysfunction deserves your RSVP.

A Story From a Friend — and a Wake-Up Call

I once had a friend who ignored red flags the way some people ignore expiration dates — she knew something was off, but she kept convincing herself it was fine.

At first, everything with her guy was sweet.
Charming. Consistent. Thoughtful.

Then things shifted.

He started making "jokes":
"Oh, you really think you can handle that promotion?"
"That dress is bold… who you trying to impress?"

It seemed small at first.
But small insults turn into big wounds when you keep allowing them.

Then he started monitoring her —
"Send me a picture of where you are."
"Why didn't you answer quicker?"

It escalated quietly.
Control always does.

And the breaking point?
At an event she wanted to take a simple photo —
just capturing a memory —
and he told her:

"This event isn't about you."

Sis… that cut deep.
The tone.
The dismissal.
The shift.

That wasn't humility.
That wasn't guidance.
That was someone shrinking her to make himself bigger.

Later, she told me:
"It's like he wanted to own me, not love me."

And that stuck with me.

Because many of us do the same thing —
we repaint red flags white because the truth hurts too much to confront.

My Own Quiet Red Flags

And let me be transparent for a second —
I'm no exception.

Red flags have shown up in my life too.

I once dated a man who crossed my boundaries so loudly it was almost unbelievable.
We barely knew each other, still getting acquainted, and suddenly:

He publicly announced we were in a relationship.
No conversation.
No consent.
No clarity.

His reasoning?
"I want everyone to know you're mine."

That wasn't romance.
That was possession dressed as passion.

Another time, I was at an event enjoying myself, wanted to take a nice photo, and I heard:

"This event is not about you."

Sis, that may seem small.
But red flags often start small —
in the tone, the attitude, the subtle attempts to dim your light.

Sometimes the biggest warning signs come in the softest voices.

Recognizing Red Flags Early

Before emotional attachment makes it harder to leave. Because once feelings get involved, clarity gets blurred.

Here are red flags you cannot excuse:

- **Constant criticism or belittling**
  You'll start shrinking yourself to fit into someone else's insecurity.

- **Controlling who you see, wear, or talk to**
  Guidance and control are not the same thing.
  You KNOW the difference.

- **Gaslighting**
  When he makes you question your memory, your reality, your sanity.

- **Explosions followed by apologies**
  The "I'm sorry" cycle always escalates.
  Always.

- **Monitoring your phone, social media, or finances**
  If he wants access because he cares, that's one thing.

- If he wants access because he's controlling — you'll feel the difference in your spirit.

- **Physical aggression — even once**
  A line crossed once is easy to cross again.

- **Financial control**
  If your dependence fuels his power, that's a trap, not love.

Let's Call Them What They Are

- Inconsistent communication

- Love bombing followed by withdrawal

- Controlling behavior masked as protection

- "Jokes" that tear you down

- Lack of accountability

- Boundary violations

- Blaming you for his behavior

- Minimizing your feelings

- Dismissing your needs

None of these are "quirks."
None are "just how he is."
None are "normal relationship ups and downs."

They are prep work for deeper harm.

You Are Not His Therapist

A man's unhealed wounds are not your responsibility.
His anger is not your assignment.
His trauma is not your ministry.

Potential without action is just a fantasy.
You're not here to rebuild a grown man from scratch.

What Real Love Looks Like

Real love doesn't require you to shrink.
Real love doesn't silence you.
Real love doesn't punish your boundaries.
Real love doesn't confuse your spirit.

Healthy love is consistent.
Peaceful.
Safe.

Healthy love waters your growth, not your anxiety.

You Don't Need Closure

Closure is a luxury. Peace is a choice.

If something feels off, that's your closure.
If someone shows you who they are, that's your warning.

Walk away with your dignity, not with explanations.

Believe the Red Flags

From now on:

> Believe the shift.
> Believe the tone.
> Believe the comment that didn't sit right.
> Believe the inconsistency.
> Believe the discomfort.

Red flags are messages from your future self.
Don't let her down.

And Sis… some red flags aren't loud at all.
They don't show up in shouting or obvious disrespect.
They show up in confusion — in the moments when someone makes you question what you saw, what you heard, or what you felt.

That's not miscommunication.
That's **mind games**.

And in the next chapter, we're going to call it what it is: **gaslighting** — the kind of manipulation that attacks your clarity and steals your peace.

Let's get into it.

HER Mirror Moment: Sis, Say It Out Loud

"I see the signs. I trust my intuition. I release anything that threatens my peace. Red flags will no longer be painted green in my world."

HER Word: Sis, Let's Reflect

Sis, it's that time again. Grab your *"Her Reflection"* journal. Be honest. Be real. This is for you.

Your Reflection Questions

1. What red flags have you ignored in past relationships, and what made you overlook them at the time?

2. When you think back, what was the very first sign that something wasn't right and how did you respond (or not respond)?

3. If you met the old you today, what red flag would you warn her about immediately?

4. What patterns do you notice in the type of red flags you've overlooked, and how can you break that cycle?

17

SIS, SOMEONE'S BEEN PLAYING MIND GAMES (GASLIGHTING)

"When someone constantly makes you question your reality, it's not love, it's control. Trust your gut, Sis. It remembers what your mind tried to forget."
— Yanique P. Walters

L̲et's start here: **You're not crazy.**

That confusion you feel? That lump in your throat when you want to speak up? That hesitation where you replay conversations in your head trying to figure out if you're overreacting? That inner war where your heart says one thing but he convinces you it's something else?

Sis… that's not miscommunication.
That's not inconsistency.
That's not "maybe I'm doing too much."
That's gaslighting.

SIS, SOMEONE'S BEEN PLAYING MIND GAMES (GASLIGHTING)

Gaslighting is emotional manipulation that makes you question your reality, your experiences, your voice, and even your worth. It's when someone twists things so smoothly that you start apologizing for the very thing they did. It's subtle, sticky, and strategic — and the most dangerous part is that it slowly makes you believe the problem is you.

Let me introduce you to Tasha.

Tasha met a guy who did everything right at first — flowers, late-night calls, compliments dripping like honey. He studied her, learned her softness, and mirrored everything she wanted. But over time, the sweetness soured.

If she brought up something that hurt her, he flipped it.
"You're too sensitive."
"You always want to argue."
"You must be imagining things — I never said that."

And the sad part? She started believing him.
She started questioning her own memory.

She apologized for her feelings.
She shrank herself to avoid "causing problems."

But you want to know the truth?
The only problem was him.

My Story: When a Community Gaslit Me

Gaslighting doesn't only happen in relationships — sometimes it comes from entire communities.

There was a time I was being stalked. I had proof. Evidence. Things that would make any sane person say, "Sis, protect yourself." But when I told the community, they made me feel like I was dramatic.
"You're imagining it."
"He's harmless."
"You're making a big deal out of nothing."

They saw the danger right in front of them and STILL told me it didn't exist.

Do you know how lonely it feels when a whole community decides your safety doesn't matter?

I left — not because I wanted to, but because I knew if anything happened to me, they would blame me instead of him. That's **communal gaslighting** — when a group invalidates your truth until even YOU start doubting your sanity.

Moral of the story:
Don't wait for permission to trust yourself.
Don't wait for disaster to justify your intuition.

Another Story: When Society Gaslights Women Daily

I'll never forget being on a bus when a man masturbated behind me and ejaculated on the floor. When I screamed for help, instead of outrage, I heard:
"You're too attractive."
"What did you expect looking that good?"

Do you see the madness?
A man violated me, yet I was blamed.

That's **social gaslighting** — when society blames women for the actions of men.

This is why women shrink.
This is why we question ourselves.
This is why we stay silent.

Because too many of us have been conditioned to believe our safety isn't a priority.

Another Romantic Example – The Manipulator Who Uses Love as a Weapon

There was a man I dated who twisted every boundary into proof that I didn't care about him.

If I said "no," he said I was cold.
If I took space, he said I didn't love him.
If I held him accountable, he said I was attacking him.

His favorite line was:
"You don't feel for me the way I feel for you."

And every time he said it, I could feel my confidence slipping.
That's how emotional manipulators work — they use your kindness against you.

The truth?
You don't love me more —
you just want more control.

I thank God I left quickly. Because someone like that doesn't stop. They just adjust until you're drained, confused, and too tired to fight back.

Different Types of Gaslighting

Sometimes we think gaslighting only happens in romantic relationships, but Sis, it has many forms:

1. Romantic gaslighting

Twisting your emotions to avoid accountability.
Denying conversations.
Calling you "dramatic," "crazy," or "paranoid."

2. Familial gaslighting

When your family invalidates your pain:
"That didn't happen."
"You're too emotional."
"You always make things worse."

3. Social gaslighting

Communities, systems, or society blaming you for what happened TO you.

4. Spiritual gaslighting

Using God or religion to manipulate you into staying in harm's way.

5. Workplace gaslighting

Coworkers or leaders dismissing your concerns and rewriting events to make you feel incompetent.

6. Self-gaslighting

The most dangerous kind — when you've been invalidated so long that you begin invalidating yourself.
"Maybe I'm being too sensitive."
"Maybe it wasn't that bad."
"Maybe I should just let it go."

Sis… you shouldn't have to talk yourself out of your own truth.

How to Protect Yourself

1. Trust your gut
Your intuition is not a lie detector — it's a life protector.

2. Document everything
Gaslighters thrive in confusion. Receipts bring clarity.

3. Talk to someone grounded
Isolation makes manipulation easier.

4. Set firm boundaries
"I don't like the way this feels" is a whole sentence.

5. Leave if necessary
You are not required to lose your sanity to keep a relationship.

6. Heal your inner voice

Gaslighting wounds your confidence deeply.

Therapy, coaching, and self-reflection help you reclaim your truth.

Sis, someone has been playing mind games with you — but the game ends today.
You are not crazy.
You are not imagining things.
You are not "too much."
You are not the problem.

Your reality is valid.
Your voice is real.
And your truth deserves respect.

In the next chapter, we will get inside the men's mind. Maybe we will understand why they do the things they do.

HER Mirror Moment: Sis, Say It Out Loud

"I am not confused. I am not dramatic. I am clear, grounded, and I trust my inner voice. Anyone who tries to dim that light is not for me."

HER Word: Sis, Lets Reflect

It's that time again. An honest moment with your *"**Her** Reflection"* journal. Grab it and reflect on the following:

Your Reflection Questions

1. Have you ever questioned your reality because of someone's words or actions?
2. What's one time your gut was right about something, even when someone tried to convince you otherwise?
3. What new boundary can you put in place to protect your peace?
4. Has someone ever made you feel "too sensitive" or "crazy" for calling out something they actually did?

SIS, HERE'S THE TRUTH I HAD TO LEARN

Sis, these are the things I wish I knew that I want you to take away from **PART THREE.**

Chapter 12: Sis, That's Not Love – That's Abuse

- Abuse isn't always loud or violent, sometimes it's silence, control, manipulation, or walking on eggshells.
- Love shouldn't make you feel afraid, small, or unsure of your worth.
- You don't have to stay to prove your loyalty, survival is not a love language.
- Being needed is not the same as being valued.
- If you constantly feel like you're the problem, take a step back, it might not be you.
- You're allowed to leave even if they didn't hit you. Emotional abuse is still abuse. It goes beyond the punches.

Chapter 13: Sis, That Man is Love Bombing You!

- Intensity isn't intimacy, slow love is usually safer love.
- Just because he says all the right things doesn't mean he's the right one.
- If it feels too good to be true in week one, then it might be.
- Real love builds over time, it doesn't rush to own you.
- Consistency matters more than chemistry.
- Someone moving fast with you doesn't mean they see your value. It might mean they see your vulnerability. Or they're trying to hide their own.

Chapter 14: Sis, He's Not Your Project

- You are not a rehab center for emotionally unavailable men.
- Loving him harder won't make him whole.
- You can support someone without sacrificing yourself.
- His healing is his responsibility, not your assignment.
- Fixing someone isn't love, it's a trauma response.
- You deserve someone who's ready, not just someone who needs you.

Chapter 15: Sis, Trust Your Intuition

- Your gut is God's whisper, listen.
- Just because you can't explain it doesn't mean it's wrong.
- When the doubt in your body is louder than the words in his mouth, take a pause and reassess.
- Stop waiting for "proof" of what you already feel.
- If something feels off, it probably is.
- Your spirit knows before your mind catches up. Trust HER.

Chapter 16: Sis, Red Flags Aren't Decorations

- A red flag is not a reason to try harder.
- Stop romanticizing dysfunction just because it's familiar.
- You're not supposed to struggle your way into being loved.
- Don't confuse passion with patterns.
- If you keep making excuses for someone, start paying attention to yourself instead.
- Red flags aren't meant to be collected, they're meant to be noticed and avoided.

Chapter 16: Sis, Someone's Been Gaslighting

- If you're always apologizing but don't know what to do, pause.
- When someone denies your reality, they're not loving you, they're controlling you.
- Gaslighting isn't confusion, it's calculated.
- If you question yourself more than you question them, then something's wrong.
- You don't owe anyone silence to keep the peace.
- Your clarity is sacred, protect it.

PART FOUR

Insight, intention, and a look inside the men's mind

We've heard your story, now let's hear theirs.

18
———

SIS, WHAT MEN REALLY THINK BUT DON'T SAY OFTEN

"A man's truth may sting, but a woman's healing begins
when she finally stops romanticizing confusion"

—Yanique P. Walters

S is… this chapter was hard to write. Not because I didn't have the words, but because I had too many. Too many emotions. Too many realizations. Too many moments where I had to pause, close my laptop, and just *breathe*. I asked men real questions. And I expected real answers. But what I didn't expect… was honesty that cut deep. Vulnerability I wasn't ready for. And clarity that made me look at *myself.* And before you brush this off like, *"Why should I care what men think?"*

I need you to pause. Breathe with me. Because whether we admit it or not, some of us have been living for their validation. We've been shrinking, bending, over-giving, and overcompensating, just to be chosen. And if we're going to tell the *whole* truth in this book, then we have to listen too. Not just to our own pain, but to the patterns. To the other side of the story. So this chapter? It's not for them. It's for us. To see clearer. To love wiser. And to stop pouring into men who never planned to pour back.

The Pressure to Provide

One of the first things the men shared was this: They *do* feel pressure to provide. Not just financially, but emotionally, mentally, and spiritually. "It's not that I don't want to love her. I do. I just don't feel like a man yet. And if I can't lead or provide, then I feel like I'm not ready for her."

That shook me. Because how many of us have taken a man's hesitation as rejection? When deep down, it was fear of not being able to *lead* us well.

Some men withdraw not because they don't care, but because they don't feel *ready*. And instead of communicating that, they go silent. They stall. They disappear. Not because they're bad men, but because they fear failing someone they actually admire.

"I won't ask a woman to build with me if my foundation is shaky. I'd rather lose her now than watch her suffer later."

That's what one man said. And as much as it sounds noble, it's also deeply telling. A man who doesn't feel secure will likely not move forward, even if you're everything he's prayed for.

Sisterly Advice:

Sis, don't build your life on a "maybe". If he's unsure, then be sure about yourself. You can support a man's growth, but you should never sit in a holding pattern, waiting to be chosen.

Acting Like a Wife Too Soon

Whew… this one. So many women, myself included, have stepped fully into "wifey mode" before a man even asked us to. And the men noticed.

"It felt like she was trying to earn me. Like she was interviewing for a job I never posted."

Ouch. But real. Some men admitted they appreciated the gestures. But most said it created discomfort or confusion. It felt rushed. Unearned. Premature. Because when you give too much too soon, before clarity, before commitment—it no longer feels like love. It feels like pressure. And pressure pushes people away.

"It felt good, but I never saw her as my woman. She just made things easy."

That one? It left a lump in my throat. Because how often do we think doing more will make him stay, when all it really does is confirm to him that he doesn't have to do much at all?

Sisterly Advice:

Sis, don't try to love a man into choosing you. Be kind, be authentic, but don't audition. Your presence is the proof. You don't need to over-give to be seen.

Staying After He Said He's Not Serious

I asked men what they thought about women who stayed around even after they said they weren't looking for anything serious. The answers broke my heart.

"I told her upfront, but she stayed… and eventually, I couldn't respect that."
Some said they appreciated the company, the affection, and the loyalty. But even then, they never saw her as "the one." And they weren't

confused about that. Sis, that's the part that hurt most: *they weren't confused.* We were.

They told us what it was. Yet, we stayed, hoping to change their mind. But in doing so, we taught them it was okay to give us less than we deserved.

Sisterly Advice:

Sis, if he says he's not ready, believe him the first time. Your love will not unlock a man's readiness. Staying after clarity is not loyalty, it's self-abandonment.

When He Keeps Sleeping With You… But Doesn't Want You

I asked the men if they'd ever kept sleeping with a woman after telling her they didn't want a relationship. Most said yes. Some said it was mutual fun. Others said it was selfish. A few admitted it was because they didn't want to be alone, but didn't want to be accountable either.

"If she keeps showing up, why would I stop taking what's being offered?"

That stung. Not because they were cruel but because they were *comfortable.* And Sis, here's the hard truth: Comfortable men rarely change. And if he's getting intimacy without responsibility, he has no reason to shift the dynamic.

Sisterly Advice:

Sis, stop offering the benefits of love without the structure of love. You are not a placeholder. You are not a trial version. If he isn't offering depth, stop giving him access to yours.

Low Confidence & Self-Worth

The men were surprisingly gentle here. They didn't bash women. But they were honest. "It's hard to love someone who doesn't love herself. You constantly feel like you're trying to prove you care… and it's never enough."

Many said they could recognize when a woman hadn't healed. Some stayed and tried to uplift her, but most eventually pulled away. Not because she wasn't lovable. But because she didn't *believe* she was. And no man can fix what you refuse to face.

Sisterly Advice:
Sis, you teach people how to treat you based on what you believe you deserve. Healing is not optional, it's foundational. Do the work for you, not just for the relationship you want.

Ghosting
Let's talk about it. I asked men why they ghosted women. And their answers were… human.

- "I didn't know how to let her down."
- "I lost interest but didn't want to hurt her."
- "She got too attached too fast."
- "I was going through stuff and couldn't handle it."

Some said they don't ghost. But most admitted they had. And here's the truth: Ghosting usually says more about *them* than it does about *you*. It's not always personal, it's often emotional immaturity, avoidance, or fear. But that doesn't make it okay.

Sisterly Advice:
Sis, silence is a sentence. Don't chase explanations from a man who didn't respect you enough to say goodbye. Your closure is in the fact that he *left*.

Emotional Shutdown

I asked the men if they've ever emotionally shut down in relationships. The answer: Yes. Many times.

- "I shut down when I feel unheard."
- "I tried to talk, but it felt pointless."
- "I stopped fighting to be understood."

Some were exhausted. Some were scared of saying the wrong thing. Others were dealing with trauma, pride, or partners who made vulnerability feel unsafe.

But here's what I learned: Most emotional shutdowns weren't the first response. They were the last straw.

Sisterly Advice:

Sis, you can't pull emotion out of someone who's decided to go numb. And once he's gone emotionally, no amount of begging can bring him back. Protect your heart, and if you need to, walk away emotionally *before* he does. But ensure that you are taking note of what they also wanted, because this is real. Men want to feel emotionally safe.

What Men Wish We Understood

This part made me tear up. Many men said they wanted to be *seen* beyond stereotypes. They wished women would stop assuming, stop performing, and just *listen*.

"We fall in love with peace," one said. "Not pressure. Not performance. Peace."

They value respect. Consistency. Safety. Not perfection. Not pretending.

They don't need a superwoman. They need someone who's *real*.

They admitted, commitment is hard when the world tells them they're disposable or unworthy, unless they have money or status.
But when a man feels safe, seen *and* respected, that's when he begins to build.

> **Sisterly Advice:**
> Sis, a good man doesn't need you to be everything. He needs you to be *you*. Peace, honesty, softness, and standards, that's what love is built on.

Now that we've heard what the men had to say and peeled back some hard truths, it's time to shift the focus back where it belongs, *on YOU*. Because Sis, you deserve more than mixed signals and emotional confusion. You deserve clarity, consistency, and love that doesn't leave you questioning yourself.

Real love? It doesn't play games. It doesn't keep you guessing. **Real love is intentional**, and in this next chapter, we're going to talk about what that actually looks like.

HER Mirror Moment: Sis, Say It Out Loud

"I no longer perform to be chosen. I stand in my worth and trust that the right love will honor it, not confuse it."

HER WORD: Sis, Let's Reflect

It's time to grab your *"Her Reflection"* journal.

I know this is a long list, but this chapter? Whew! It was layered, honest, and probably stirred up some things you've been carrying in silence. We touched on truth, timing, self-worth, and the kind of love that leaves you questioning your value. Before you move on, take a moment to unpack it all.

Your Reflection Questions

1. Have you ever paused your progress just to wait on a man to catch up?
2. What part of you believed you had to do more to be loved?
3. Have you exchanged your body for emotional connection?
4. What is one part of you that still needs to be loved better?
5. Did you feel like you were carrying the relationship emotionally?
6. Are you showing up with your true self or a version you think will impress him?

19

SIS, REAL LOVE IS INTENTIONAL

"Real love doesn't leave you guessing. It doesn't ask you to perform. It shows up, consistently, with clarity and care."

– Yanique P. Walters

Have you ever sat there wondering, "What are we even doing?" Like... nothing's clear. Y'all are hanging out, but there's no real progress being made. Well...

After the pandemic, I decided it was time for this queen to find her king. I was home, eating right, glowing skin, no sunburn, no junk food, I was looking good! I was ready to touch outside again and see what the world had to offer. So, I took some bomb photos, created my online profile, and got back on the dating scene.

Whew, Chile... It was interesting. Scary. Weird. Awkward. I dealt with it all. But the best part? I learned to sit across the table from a man and discern his intentions, who meant what they said, and who was just saying things to pass time.

Now listen, I ain't no expert, I'm just sharing from my own experience and from conversations I've had with men who kept it real with me.

Let's be honest: men who are intentional usually make it known right out the gate.

If you meet a man and he says he's "going with the flow," "open to whatever," or "just taking things easy," please, sis, do not take that man seriously.

That is a dangerous game. And you'll lose woefully

Yes, occasionally, a man gets out here playing and then realizes he doesn't want to lose a good woman. But usually? That's the exception, not the rule.

Let me give you an example.

I met a guy who tried to get me to spend the night with him on the first date by offering me two outfits. He literally said, "I bought you two outfits, but they're back at the hotel. If you don't mind, you can come back with me."

Sir, be for real.

That was a no.

His intentions were clear. Could it have turned into something more? Maybe. But from that first move, I already knew where his priorities were.

When I spoke to men, they told me straight up: women are the gatekeepers of their bodies.

If a woman says she's not having sex until marriage, or until there's a real commitment, and the man walks away? Good. That's your filter.

If he stays and tries to pressure her into changing her mind? That's also your answer.

Do not use sex out of fear of losing him. Because if sex is the only thing keeping him, then you never had him to begin with.

What Intentionality Looks Like

- A man who's truly intentional about you will:
- Value you as a person
- Enjoy your company
- Want to know every little detail about you
  And honestly? He'll be a little high off your energy—just being around you will be enough

Watch for the Patterns

Now, let's talk about patterns.

If you've been seeing someone for months and still haven't met his friends or family, that's a red flag.

If he only ever wants to come to your place and you've never been to his? Sis, that's suspicious.

If he only calls at night, shows no interest in what matters to you, and y'all barely talk unless you're physically together, he doesn't really like you that much.

When a man is intentional, there's:

- Clear communication
- Consistent actions (not just sweet words)
- Effort without pressure
- Thoughtful planning and vision
- Emotional availability
- Accountability and follow-through

An Example of Intentional Love

Let me tell you about one man I dated long-distance.

From the beginning, he was intentional. He communicated openly, told me what he was looking for, and we agreed to talk nightly. We even made monthly plans to visit each other and do fun things together. He planned all the dates, cooked for me, and made sure I was good.

That, Sis, is what intentionality looks like.

We didn't work out long-term for other reasons, but it wasn't because he didn't make his intentions clear.

Sis, If You're Still Wondering... He's Probably Not

If a man leaves you confused, it's likely because he's okay with you feeling that way.

Let's stop chasing men who are emotionally unavailable, inconsistent, avoid accountability, or only want to "vibe" with no direction.

Alright Sis, now that we've broken down what intentional love looks like, let's flip the script and ask the men: **what actually makes a woman stand out?** In the next chapter, we're talking about that defining moment, when a man knows she's not just someone he's dating, but the one he wants to build with. Let's hear how they knew... and what we can learn from it.

HER Mirror Moment: Sis, Say It Out Loud

"I no longer settle for confusion. I attract clarity, consistency, and love that aligns with my worth."

HER Word: Sis, Let's Reflect

Sis, grab your *"Her Reflection"* journal. This chapter was short but full of real moments we've all experienced. We've glamorized chemistry and ignored confusion.

We've made excuses for "chilling" when we deserve to be cherished. If this stirred something in you, don't rush past it. Sit with these questions and get honest about how you've been showing up, and what you will no longer tolerate.

Your Reflection Questions

1. What does intentional love look and feel like for you?
2. What patterns have you accepted that made you doubt your worth?
3. How will you show up for yourself differently from now on?
4. Where in your life have you been settling for attention instead of genuine care?

20

SIS, WHAT MAKES A MAN CHOOSE "HER" AND NOT OTHERS

"Peace is not about silence, it's about safety. And the right man will feel safest with the version of you that's soft, real, and whole."

— *Yanique P. Walters*

I had the opportunity to sit down with a few married men, and the burning question on my mind was: "How did you know she was the one?" The general answer from every single one of them? **"She was my peace."**

Now Sis, before this conversation, I hated when men said they wanted a woman to "be their peace." Like… are you being our peace? Are we just waking up acting crazy for fun? Or are you giving us reasons to come at you?

But I listened. And what they said made me pause.

They explained that some women genuinely love drama, or are constantly on edge, and that kind of energy doesn't usually lead to partnership.

Now Sis, I know a lot of us have had that moment where we've looked at a man's choice and thought, "Really? Her?"

It's easy to assume he's just out here flaunting the "baddies," but will settle down with the so-called "plain Jane."

But what I heard from the men I spoke with challenged that belief.

They said:
"It wasn't about her looks—it was how I felt around her. She was my peace."

And Sis, that's powerful. It means we don't have to twist ourselves into society's version of "sexy" or "perfect" to be chosen. What matters most is how someone experiences your presence. Your energy. Your consistency. Your heart.

One guy shared that:
"She didn't pressure me. She was just consistent."

It's not about dimming your light to fit a mold; it's about letting your real self-shine and trusting that the right one will feel it.

What "Peace" Actually Looks Like

So naturally, I had to ask: What does "peace" even mean to y'all?

Here's what they said:

- She supported them emotionally

- She let them vent when they were having a hard day
- She didn't blow up over small things
- She knew how to respectfully communicate disagreement
- She created space for honesty without judgment

One guy told me that when he and his wife disagree, they usually smile through it. They've never had a big blow-up. It's just two adults working through things with grace.

Another man shared a moment that sealed the deal for him:

He was distraught after being denied a job. He called her, and she didn't try to fix it. She just said, "Do you want to meet me at the park?" They sat for two hours while he vented, and she just listened. He said: *"The support I felt in that moment made me realize she was the one."*

Another man admitted that he had been out here, dating multiple women. But when he met his now-wife, she made him want to be a better man. He didn't want to lose her. That's when he realized all the other women had to go.

It's Not About Submission, It's About Synergy

Let me be clear: these men aren't saying women should lose their discernment or ignore their intuition. But constant fussing, fighting, and power struggles? That rarely leads to a ring.

They also said the woman they chose allowed them to lead but still taught them things in a way that made it feel like their idea. One man said: *"There's a way to teach without blaming."*

He explained that his wife is a boss in the outside world, an IT manager, making moves. But when she comes home, she switches gears. She doesn't bring that same energy into the relationship. She shows up for him as his partner, not his competition.

And yes, they said it loud and clear:
Men want to be with feminine women.

Being hard and tough 24/7 might keep you protected, but it's not what most men find inviting. Vulnerability, they said, is a woman's superpower. Use it wisely. Speak from your heart. Say how you feel without attacking. Use "I" statements instead of blame. And please, don't compare him to your ex.

Whew. I remember doing that once, and he hit me with:
"Well, where is he now?"

Whew, Chile. That one stung, but it was the truth.

Why do we move on and still expect our ex from our current partner?

Teach a man how to love you, yes, but do it with compassion, not correction.

The Bottom Line? Peace Over Performance

Men want peace. They deal with chaos out in the world. They want to come home to joy, not someone yelling about the toilet seat being up.

But sis, don't lose yourself trying to become what you think a man wants.

SIS, YOU ARE HER

You are already enough. You don't need to become someone else to be chosen. You just need to become aligned with the love you desire and just wait for the one who's truly ready to give it to you.

One of the main reasons relationships fail is that we don't take the time to vet these men. We're saying "yes" after one week and posting "my other half" before we even know if he likes dogs or pays his bills on time.

Be for real. That's not your other half, Sis. That's a whole pizza—you done sliced it eight ways in six months.

Slow down. Ask questions. Protect your peace. Let your standards speak louder than your desire to be chosen. I say this with love because I've been there. He asked me to be his girl and I jumped at it—just for it to end a few weeks later. Why? Because we didn't know each other. Or maybe he never planned to stay.

You deserve more than just "potential." You deserve consistency. You deserve love that doesn't require suffering first. Let's cut the pattern. Let's raise the standard. You're not too picky, you're just finally learning your worth.

Now that we've unpacked what makes a man recognize "the one," it's time to flip the lens back on *us*. Because knowing what men value is one thing, but making sure our standards aren't rooted in fantasy, fear, or desperation? That's the real work. In the next chapter, we're going to talk about expectations, alignment, and how to build standards that actually serve the love you deserve.

You are not a placeholder. You are the prize. And from this chapter forward, we're acting like it. But while you wait for what's meant for you, let me remind you, being single isn't a punishment, it's preparation. Let's break that down next.

HER Mirror Moment: Sis, Say It Out Loud

"I am the kind of woman who makes love feel safe, peaceful, and purposeful. The one who is chosen won't have to question my worth — he'll recognize it."

HER WORD: Sis, Let's Reflect

Alright Sis, before you flip to the next chapter, pause. This is your moment. Go ahead and grab your *"Her Reflection"* journal, your favorite pen, light a candle if you want... and let's reflect for real. This chapter isn't just tea, it is truth. And now, it's time to turn that truth inward and ask yourself the kind of questions that help you grow, not shrink.

Your Reflection Questions

1. What do you think it means to be 'the one'?
2. Have you ever chased validation from someone who wasn't ready to choose you?
3. What qualities do you bring into a relationship that reflect love, peace, and partnership?
4. Are you chasing a future with someone who doesn't even see one with you?

SIS, HERE IS THE TRUTH I HAD TO LEARN

Sis, These Are the Things I Wish I Knew That I Want You to Take Away from **PART FOUR**

Chapter 18: Sis, A Look Inside The Male Mind

- Men do feel deeply — they just express it differently.
- Vulnerability isn't just a woman's language — some men speak it fluently, too.
- The right man will *want* to communicate, reflect, and show up.
- Real men are not intimidated by your strength, just your unwillingness to settle.
- Sometimes, the answers you need come from asking the hard questions and listening without defense.

Chapter 19: Sis, Know When He Is Being Intentional

- Real love doesn't just happen, it's *built* with intention, grace, and daily right choices.
- A man who loves you will pursue clarity, not confusion.
- You don't have to guess if it's real, real love will show up consistently.
- Being chosen means nothing if you're not being honored in the process.
- You're not asking for too much, you're simply asking for what's *meant* for you.

Chapter 20: How Did You Know She Was the One?

- Men value peace, and peace doesn't mean silence, it means safety.
- You don't have to perform to be chosen. Your *presence* is the gift.
- The right one will recognize your softness as a strength, not a weakness.
- A woman who leads with love, not control, leaves an imprint that lasts.
- You are not too strong, too loud, or too much, you're just not for someone who wants less.

PART FIVE

Becoming HER (Identity, Gratitude & Alignment)

This is where the shift happens.

21

SIS, SINGLE-LIFE IS NOT PUNISHMENT

"Being single isn't a season of lack, it's a sacred season of alignment. I'd rather wait whole than settle half-loved."
— *Yanique P. Walters*

They say the devil finds work for idle hands, and chile, one afternoon he surely gave me plenty. I was lying in bed, scrolling and reflecting, when I found myself in a "why am I still single" spiral.

A close friend of mine had just shared that he was getting married, and I was truly happy for him. But the joy was followed by a whisper: *Why not me?* Everyone around me seemed to be moving forward, and here I was... stuck. Or so I thought.

So, I texted him in my spiral:

"Hey my friend, just here thinking… You're getting married in a few weeks, and I'm still in the same position you met me three years ago. Single and lonely."

His response? Whew, it shook me:

"Hey my friend, I have a message for you… I'm so impressed with your growth since we became friends. You've bought a home. You've built a brand. You've traveled the world. You've increased your earnings. You wrote a book. And most importantly, your son is healed. **YOU ARE BLESSED.***"*

That message snatched me back. It reminded me that sometimes we overlook the masterpiece we've already created because we're focused on the one piece that hasn't clicked yet.

And the truth? He was right. I *had* been building. I was just too busy counting what I didn't have to celebrate what I did.

So what was I doing in my single season?

- **I bought a home.** You don't have to wait for a couple's mortgage to create stability. You can plant roots now.
- **I traveled.** I saw new places, met new people, and experienced life on my own terms.
- **I poured into my son.** This season gave me space to focus on his healing and growth.
- **I prioritized myself;** My health, my peace, my goals—all things I might have sacrificed if I'd been tangled in the wrong relationship.

Whoever said being single was the end of the world lied. Because babyyyy, life is still good, full of adventures!

Let's Shift the Narrative

Being single isn't a punishment. It's not a curse or a failure. It's a season of alignment, clarity, growth, and preparation. It's a blessing. It's your time to rise.

But I get it, society tells us otherwise. We've been fed so many lies about singleness:

- "If you're single, something must be wrong with you."

- "You better hurry up; your biological clock is ticking."

- "You're too picky. Lower your standards."

Sis, those aren't facts, they're fear tactics. And they're designed to pressure women into settling, rushing, or second-guessing themselves. But not us, not anymore. You're not broken. You're not behind. You're building.

Love Right, Not Fast

When I got my divorce, I thought I'd be in a new relationship in no time. But this dating world? Whew, it's a battlefield.

My goal isn't just to be in a relationship; it's to be loved right. That means being intentional, being prayerful, being patient.

I see people asking for "Ciara's prayer," but instead of copying someone else's list, why not build yours? Ask God for what you truly want, not what looks good on someone else. And if it feels like God is taking His time, maybe it's because He's crafting your man with care. You're not being delayed, you're being prepared.

Don't Chase Perfection

Let me hit you with an analogy: the "Husband Store."

A woman walks in. The first floor has cute, kind men. She thinks, "I can do better." The second floor has cute, kind men with good jobs. Still, "I can do better." The third floor has all that and more. But she keeps going up. By the time she reaches the top floor, it's empty except for a sign that says: *"This floor exists only to prove women can never be satisfied."*

Sis, don't get caught chasing perfection. No one is flawless, and neither are you. Write down your non-negotiables and stick to them. But don't nitpick the small stuff. For me, I used to have a thing about men's voices. If it wasn't deep and masculine, I couldn't deal. But really? Am I going to block my blessing over vocal cords? Chile… we're working on that.

Live While You Wait

Being single gives you freedom:

- To travel without compromise.
- To dive deep into friendships and passions.
- To explore who you are and what you want.

You're not stuck, you're spacious. You're not behind, you're becoming.

Every March, I take a birthday trip. Bali one year, Colombia the next. Sometimes I bring old friends, sometimes new ones. Each trip reminds me of how much life there is to enjoy, partner or not.

SIS, YOU ARE HER

So don't sit at home waiting for Prince Charming. Sis, he doesn't have your address. Get out and meet the world halfway.

You're Building, Not Waiting

Sis, you're not waiting for a man, you're creating a life. There's a big difference between waiting for love and preparing for love.

And yes, family pressure is real. The aunties with "When are you getting married?" or "Don't you want kids?" Yes, I do. But on God's timing, not theirs. Don't let anyone rush you into choosing wrong just to say you have a man. Instead, use this time to:

- Go back to school.
- Start a business.
- Build your savings.
- Get to know yourself so well that you become the partner you're seeking.
- Build solid and quality relationships

When I'm single, I'm productive. My mind is clearer. I can write, travel, dream, and breathe. Staying busy in your single season is a gift. Because when you're idle, loneliness can whisper, and that's when you risk spinning the block on a man who belonged back in chapter two.

Loneliness may creep in sometimes, but don't mistake it for being unlovable. It's just a feeling, and feelings pass.

Being single is not punishment, it's a time to grow stamina. Don't be in a hurry to build with someone just to tick the 'married' box. A brick not properly laid and watered will definitely result in a collapsed home when the winds and tides come blowing. It's preparation for the next season of your life. It's a reminder that you are already whole, already worthy. But wholeness isn't about performing or pretending to be who you think someone else will love. It's about being true to yourself. Let's explore what that kind of authenticity looks like in the next chapter.

HER Mirror Moment: Sis, Say It Out Loud

"I am not waiting to be loved. I am whole. My season of singleness is not punishment; it is preparation, elevation, and freedom."

HER Word: Sis, Let's Reflect

It's that time again. Find a quiet space, grab your *"Her Reflection"* journal, and be brutally honest with yourself. No sugarcoating, no filters, just you are getting real about this single season and what it's teaching

Your Reflection Questions

1. What messages have you internalized about being single?
2. In what ways have you allowed fear or shame to influence how you feel about this season?
3. What goals, dreams, or habits can you focus on while you are single?
4. How can you use this season of singleness to strengthen your relationship with yourself?

you.

22

SIS, BE TRUE TO WHO YOU ARE

"Authenticity is the daily practice of letting go of who we think we're supposed to be and embracing who we are."
— Brené Brown

Let me say this loud and clear: **there's peace in being yourself.**

Not the curated version. Not the masked-up, performance-ready version. Just you.

In a world full of opinions, unspoken rules, and silent pressure to conform, choosing authenticity is an act of courage. I know it's not always easy. Sometimes, the world makes you feel like being yourself is too loud, too soft, too bold, too emotional, too much, or not enough.

But sis, **if healing is your goal, authenticity must be your commitment.**

Pretending will drain you. Performing will bury you. But being real? That's where freedom lies.

When I Cared "Zero" (But Not Really)

Back in my twenties, my motto was *"I care zero."* It was in my email signature, plastered across my social media statuses — my personal brand before I even knew what branding was. At the time, it was my coping mechanism, the mantra I used to push through pain and condition myself to keep moving. On the surface, it looked true. I was expressive, vibrant, fearless, and even a little rebellious. But the truth? I did care. I just didn't *perform* for anyone's comfort. That season taught me something valuable: when I stopped trying to impress people, I actually started impressing myself.

But as I stepped into the corporate world, that shifted. Not because I stopped being true to myself, but because I became aware of how I was being perceived. I wasn't just representing *me* anymore; I was representing an entire company. So yes, I adjusted. I refined. I adapted. But here's what I didn't do: I didn't fake it.

I've had moments where I was told things like;
"Just smile and say yes."
"Tone it down so others feel more comfortable."
"Don't stand out too much, it might ruffle feathers."

But that has never been me. I'm kind, I'm respectful, I'm a team player, but I'm also real. If I smile with you, it's genuine. If I clap for you, I mean it. Because I truly believe **authenticity doesn't need to be sacrificed for professionalism**, they can coexist.

Wearing the Mask Comes at a Cost

Let's be honest: constantly pretending takes a toll. When you spend eight hours smiling when you're hurting, agreeing when you're uncertain, or shrinking when you should speak, **your soul starts to suffocate.** You go home feeling out of alignment. You replay conversations and wonder, *"Why didn't I just speak up?"*

Here's the truth:

- You can be professional without being passive.
- You can be kind without being fake.
- You can be coachable without abandoning your core.

There's a difference between **growing** and **people-pleasing**. Don't confuse the two.

Don't sit in silence just to keep the peace. Don't hold in your ideas just to appear agreeable. You deserve to have a voice, and your team deserves to hear it.

Growth Is Still Required

Now let's be clear, being authentic isn't a hall pass for poor behavior. It doesn't mean saying, *"That's just how I am,"* when there's room for growth. It means being self-aware, accepting yourself, doing the work, and still showing up as your whole self.

If you know there are areas where you can improve, maybe communication, emotional intelligence, or navigating conflict, seek help. Find a coach. Ask for feedback.

Authenticity + accountability = power.

And remember my "I care zero" phase? That version of me wasn't afraid to speak up, even if it was uncomfortable. Somewhere between then and now, I've learned you can keep that boldness and still pair it with wisdom, respect, and intentionality.

Authenticity Builds Stronger Teams

Being true to yourself isn't about resisting feedback or refusing to adapt, it's about showing up with honesty *and* a willingness to grow. When we bring our real selves to the table, we invite others to do the same, and that's where trust is built.

It's also about balance. There's a time to speak and a time to listen. A time to lead with your perspective, and a time to lean into the wisdom of others. True authenticity isn't rigid, it's flexible enough to collaborate, open enough to consider other viewpoints, and grounded enough to stand firm when it matters most.

When you combine authenticity with respect, curiosity, and a team-first mindset, you don't just protect your peace, you contribute to a culture where everyone feels safe to contribute theirs too.

Real Quick, Let's Talk Social Media

While authenticity matters at work, it's just as important in how you show up online.

As someone who creates content online, I've seen firsthand how people, especially women, dim themselves out of fear. Fear that a picture at the beach might cost them an opportunity. Fear that a dance video might be misinterpreted. Fear that being human online is somehow "unprofessional."

Sis, let me be real; **Context matters.**
If you're at the beach, a swimsuit makes sense. If you're at brunch in a sundress, that's normal. We can't live in fear of being seen as *too much* when we're simply being human. But we also have to remember: **presentation is powerful.**

You don't need to overshare, but don't feel like you need to disappear either.

Here's my advice:

- **Post with purpose.** Ask yourself, does this align with the version of me I'm proud of?
- **Keep it classy, not filtered beyond recognition.**
- **Draw the line between private and personal.** Not everyone needs access to your every moment, but that doesn't mean hiding who you are.
- **Separate work and play**, but don't lose yourself in the process.

Stop Apologizing for Existing

You are not too loud, too ambitious, too real, or too vibrant.
You are not a threat just because you don't shrink.

You are allowed to be kind, confident, professional, and proud. So, sis, be HER.

SIS, YOU ARE HER

The healed HER. The honest HER. The authentic HER.

Because the world doesn't need another copy-paste version of someone else. It needs you.

When you try to live someone else's life, you not only insult your maker but also deprive the world of all the unique goodness only you were created to share.

Living in your truth is powerful, but even more powerful is recognizing what's already working. The moment you begin to love who you are, is the moment you start noticing all the little things you once took for granted.

Because when you show up as your authentic self, with your flaws and all, you start to see the beauty in your journey. And that's where gratitude comes in. Sis, no matter what you've been through, there is still something to be grateful for. Let's talk about that next.

HER Mirror Moment: Sis, Say It Out Loud

"I am free to be fully me. I honor my truth without apology. I grow without losing myself. I am original. I don't fake it."

HER Word: Sis, Lets Reflect

Sis, this is your moment to keep it real with yourself. Grab your "**Her Reflection**"journal and get honest about the ways you've hidden, shrunk, or pretended to be someone you're not, and then write down what it would look like to show up as your full, unapologetic self.

Your Reflection Questions

1. In what ways have you been performing instead of being your full, authentic self?

2. What's one thing you want to say or do more often, but you've been afraid it won't be accepted?

3. How can you start showing up more fully while still honoring your responsibilities?

4. When was the last time you silenced your truth to keep the peace, and how did it make you feel?

23

SIS, GRATITUDE IS A MUST

"Gratitude doesn't mean everything is perfect. It means you choose to see the gift, even in the growing."
— *Yanique P. Walters*

S is, I know... it's hard to feel grateful when life is throwing you curveballs left, right, and center. Like, what exactly am I supposed to be thankful for when I'm crying in my car, eating French fries for dinner and making ice cream my comfort meal?

But here's the truth, that's actually the perfect time to practice gratitude. Gratitude isn't about ignoring your pain or pretending everything's fine. It's about choosing to focus on what's still good, even when everything feels like it's falling apart.

When Gratitude Found Me

In 2019, I was going through my divorce. I was pregnant. Living in a whole new country with no family, no close friends, just me and my belly, trying to figure life out. My world felt like it was crashing down. Some days, I legit wanted to pack my bags and head back to Jamaica. I'd stare at my suitcase like, *"So... we doing this or nah?"*

And then came the ANTs. Not the insects, but the **Automatic Negative Thoughts** Dr. Daniel Amen talked about. Those little mental pests whispered, *"You're a failure," "You're not good enough," "This will never get better."* And for weeks, I let them move in rent-free.

My grandma was my lifeline. I'd call her daily just to vent. "Yanique, everything gonna be alright, baby," she'd say. And it helped, until I hung up. Then bam! The ANTs were back, crawling all over my peace.

It was one of the hardest times of my life. I felt defeated, confused, stuck and I really felt like a failure.

The Shift: Gratitude as a Lifestyle

One day, I heard Oprah talking about gratitude. And not the "say thanks when someone passes the salt" kind of way. She spoke about gratitude as a lifestyle. Something clicked.

I had always heard people say "Give thanks" at church or after borrowing sugar from a neighbor. But Oprah broke it down—the *benefits* of gratitude:

- A better mood
- Stronger friendships
- Less stress

- Healthier body
- More optimism
- Even career growth and networking skills

And I thought… wait a minute. So just by being thankful, my life can shift? Say less.

That day, I went looking for a gratitude journal. I wanted a place to list what I was thankful for, reflect on my day, and write down what I was looking forward to. I couldn't find one that felt like me, so I created one. Yup, I designed and published my very own gratitude journal and made it available on Amazon for ya'll to document your gratitude too. Sharing is caring, right?

Sis, that decision definitely changed everything.

What Gratitude Did For Me

Once I started practicing gratitude, my perspective shifted. My problems didn't magically disappear, but they felt smaller. Blessings started showing up in little ways, a free meal in the drive-thru, someone covering my groceries, unexpected kindness from strangers.

My mood lifted. My confidence returned. People were drawn to my energy, because gratitude has a way of radiating out of you.

The best part? My job ended up buying copies of the gratitude journal I created for everyone on my team. Over 300 copies! Imagine that what started as a tool to save me ended up serving others too.

Catching the ANTs

Now, let's be real. The ANTs still try to creep in. But gratitude gave me tools to fight back. Here's what I do whenever they show up:

- **Ask questions**: "Is this 100% true? What proof do I have?"
- **Counter with truth**: Replace "I'll never get the job I want" with "I'm preparing for the right opportunity at the right time."
- **Release it**: Write the thought down then tear it up or burn it. Dramatic? Maybe. But healing? Absolutely.

The more I practiced this, the more I realized something powerful: **you are what you think.** Your mind is the engine, and your actions follow. If your thoughts are full of doubt and fear, your life will reflect that. If your thoughts are rooted in gratitude and hope, your life will reflect that too.

A Thank You Moment

Before I close this chapter, let me practice what I preach. To my grandma, thank you for every prayer. To Aunt Ingrid, Mommy, Latoya, Shakara, Tamara, and Renee—you held space for me when I couldn't hold myself. To my friend Michael—you saw me when I felt invisible. Thank you.

Those moments of love reminded me that even when everything else felt shaky, gratitude could ground me.

Sis, Try This Today

Gratitude isn't about pretending your pain doesn't exist. It's about refusing to let pain be the *only* story you tell.

SIS, YOU ARE HER

So, here's your challenge:

- Write down 3 things you're grateful for today.
- Tell one person "thank you."
- Speak life over yourself. Out loud.

Because Sis, gratitude makes room for joy. Gratitude silences the ANTs. Gratitude opens doors you didn't even know were waiting for you.

So go ahead, say thank you. To someone. To God. To yourself.

Because the reality is this: even the tiniest practice of gratitude can loosen the grip of pain you've been carrying. And when that pain starts to lift, it leaves you with a question: *Who are you without it?* If answering that feels hard right now, don't worry. Let's unpack it together in the next chapter...

HER Mirror Moment: Sis, Say It Out Loud

"I choose gratitude even in uncertainty. I see blessings in small moments. I attract peace, favor, and joy because I choose to focus on what's good"

HER WORD: Sis, Lets Reflect

Gratitude isn't just about feeling good, it's about shifting your focus from what's missing to what's present. It's about grounding yourself in the now, even if the now feels messy. So, before you write, pause. Breathe deeply. Let your heart settle. This moment is yours. No pressure to be perfect, just be honest. Let's take inventory of what's still good, who's shown up for you, and even what your challenges might be trying to teach you.

Your Reflection Questions

1. Three things you're grateful for today (no matter how small).

2. One person you want to thank or appreciate and why:

3. One challenge you're facing and the lesson(s) it might be teaching you.

4. If you're feeling fancy, text or call that person you're grateful for today. Your words might be exactly what their heart needs.

24

SIS, WHO ARE YOU WITHOUT THE PAIN?

"You are not what hurt you. You are who you became when
you decided to heal."

— Yanique P. Walters

Here's a question I didn't know how to answer for a long time.
Not "What do you do?"
Not "Who do you love?"
But this:

"Who are you… without the pain?"

Because for most of my life, pain had a front-row seat in everything I did. It shaped how I walked, talked, loved, stayed quiet, or fought to be heard. My confidence, my relationships, my dreams — all of it got filtered through the lens of what I had been through.

And truthfully? I didn't realize I had let my pain become my identity.

I was the strong one. The dependable one. The one who'd always been through some mess but still showed up smiling. I wore that strength like a badge... but underneath it?

My mind was stretched thin in ways I didn't even recognize at the time.

Somewhere along the line, I stopped dreaming. I stopped creating. I stopped being me. I became roles: the fixer, the giver, the survivor, the one who always knew how to bounce back.

And the more I looked at it, the more I realized something else — something deeper.

Helping others brought me joy and fulfillment. I loved being the person who could show up, solve something, support someone. It made me feel useful. Worthy. Connected. And that was something I learned from my mom. She was happiest when she was helping somebody, and I think I inherited that part of her.

But the downside?

When someone no longer needed my help, I didn't feel like I had much value to them anymore. If I wasn't fixing something, carrying something, or saving something, I didn't know what I meant to them. It felt like my identity disappeared the moment the need disappeared.

And sis, that hit me hard — not having control, not being asked, not being "the one they leaned on."

Sometimes I wonder if that's why my relationship with my mom is the way it is... maybe she never felt like I needed her. And that's the same feeling I battled — the quiet fear that without being the helper, the fixer, the backbone...

SIS, YOU ARE HER

I wasn't enough.

Are you like this too?
Do people depend on you heavily — and even though you complain about it, deep down... you love the feeling of being needed?
Does your worth feel tied to what you do for others?

Sis... that's not love.
That's identity tied to labor.
And it will drain you until you have nothing left for yourself.

And that's where this question first humbled me:
Who am I without pain?

Because sometimes life gets so heavy, so busy, so demanding...
that you don't even recognize yourself anymore.

Motherhood and Identity Loss
Becoming a mom changes your identity. Everything you do becomes centered around your child, and somewhere in that beautiful chaos, you slowly lose pieces of yourself.

After having my son, my weekends, my downtime, my spare moments — all of it was dedicated to him. Playing together. Trips to the park. Movie nights. Everything revolved around his world.

And while those moments were precious, one day I realized something painful:

I no longer knew what I liked.

People will say, "That's normal. That's just motherhood."
But says who?

Yes, we are mothers — but we are still women.
Motherhood should expand you, not erase you.

I remember being at a moms' event where everyone went around the room answering:

"What do you do for fun?"
"What do you enjoy outside of being a mother?"

Most of the mothers in that room could not answer those questions. I remember the host asked a lady head on: "Who are you?" She said, "I am a mother."
The host said, "No… let's start over. Who are you?"

She tried again: "I am—" and stopped. She couldn't answer it.
And when it got to me, same… **silence.**

My throat tightened.
My mind went blank.
Every answer I had was connected to my son — not to **ME.**

And that's how identity slips away:
When we have a fixer mentality, **you know who you are for everyone else… but you have no idea who you are for yourself.**

Dating and Identity Loss

And motherhood wasn't the only place this showed up.

Someone once asked me on a date, "So what do you like to do?"
And sis… I froze.
Because honestly? My world had revolved around survival, responsibilities, and being "strong."

But what did **I**, Yanique, actually enjoy?

SIS, YOU ARE HER

He kept asking:

"What do you like to do for fun?"
"Where do you go in your spare time?"
"What kind of food do you like?"

My heart pounded.
My skin burned.
I wanted to slide under the table.

Because suddenly, painfully, clearly…

I didn't know myself anymore.

By the end of the date, I wasn't tired of him — I was tired of me.
I cried in my car because I realized I had completely lost my identity.

The Breakdown That Became My Breakthrough

Sis, survival mode will trick you into thinking you're okay because you're functioning.

You're working.
Showing up.
Carrying everything.
Doing what needs to be done.

But functioning is NOT living.

Somewhere in the middle of doing everything for everyone else, you forget the version of you who used to laugh from her belly… who used to dream boldly… who used to do things simply because they made her feel alive.

Healing starts the moment you whisper:

"Wait… I miss me."

The Promise I Made to Myself

When the New Year rolled around, I made a resolution:

I was going to find myself again.

I started doing solo adventures.
I bought a camera and took photography lessons.
I joined the gym.
I went to the movies alone.
I took myself out to eat.
I even had a drink alone (because sometimes sis… a margarita is self-care).

Choosing myself felt strange at first.
I felt guilty spending money on me.
Guilty taking up space.
Guilty doing things that didn't benefit anyone but Yanique.

But with every small decision, I felt pieces of myself coming back.

Confidence isn't built in one big leap.
It's built in the small choices — the ones where you say:

"Today, I matter too."

I Want the Same Awakening for You

Sis, don't let pain be the thief of your identity.
You are more than what hurt you.
You are more than the roles life forced you into.
You are more than who you had to be to survive.

And if anyone ever asks you what kind of food you like, please —
don't forget your inner foodie.

But before you rediscover who you are becoming,
you must first get honest about who you lost along the way. Healing requires reflection. It requires giving yourself permission to explore the parts of you that got buried under responsibility, heartbreak, obligation, and the strength you never asked for.

So let's slow down for a minute.
Let's peel back the layers gently.
Let's meet the woman underneath the pain — the one God created before life tried to rewrite your story.

Now, Let's Do This Activity

Before we move forward, pause. Breathe.
And give yourself permission to explore **YOU** again — not the version molded by survival, responsibility, or heartbreak, but the woman underneath it all.

Write down the things you enjoyed doing when you were a free-spirited version of yourself.

Ask yourself:

• What do you love simply because you love it?
• What brings you joy that doesn't depend on anyone else?
• What dreams did you bury because someone made you feel like you were "too much"?
• When was the last time you did something not to heal, not to survive, but to feel alive?

You've come this far — peeling back layers of pain, identity, and truth. But healing isn't just about uncovering what hurt you...

It's about owning what you do next.

Because before we talk about attracting what you truly deserve, there's one more question we need to answer:

Have you taken accountability for your part in the story?

Because sis...
Healing isn't only about what happened to you.
It's about the choices you're willing to make now.

Let's talk about accountability next.

HER Mirror Moment: Sis, Say It Out Loud

"I am not defined by my pain(s), my past, or my patterns. I am the lessons I've learned, the strength I've gained, and the joy I choose to create. I am healing, I am evolving, and I am allowed to rewrite my story without carrying the scars as my identity."

HER Word: Sis, Let's Reflect

Now it's time to grab your *"Her Reflection"* journal and reflect. This isn't about getting the answers right, it's about getting honest with yourself.

You deserve to know who you are beyond the pain. Let's start there.

Your Reflection Questions

1. Without the weight of your past, how would you describe yourself at your core—the woman you are when no one is watching?

2. Who are you outside the roles you've had to play (the fixer, the strong one, the survivor)? What's left when you put those roles down?

3. What parts of you have been shaped by pain, and do you want to keep carrying those parts forward?

4. If you were no longer trying to prove you're worthy of love, what would you do differently, starting today?

25

SIS, TAKE ACCOUNTABILITY

"Healing starts when blame ends. Accountability isn't shame,
it's power in your own hands."
— *Yanique P. Walters*

S is, I know this chapter might sting a little. Accountability isn't everyone's favorite topic. It might make you want to skip ahead to something more comforting, but if you're serious about healing, we can't skip this step.

Let me share something with you.

When I started writing this book, I reached out to a group of men for my survey. One of those men was my ex. As I read through the responses, I could see our relationship in his words. I was surprised at myself; I read without getting defensive. This was him sharing how things affected him. And while he was definitely not without fault (because chile, he definitely disappointed me) I had to admit…I wasn't without fault either.

Well.. I put on my grown-woman hat and reached out to him, not to rekindle anything, but to take ownership for the role I played in the relationship. It wasn't easy, but it was necessary for my healing.

And that's when it hit me: **accountability is the grown-woman work**.
The *"let me pause and check myself"* work.
The *"I know I've been hurt, but where did I cause hurt too?"* work.

This isn't about blaming yourself for everything. It's about freeing yourself from patterns that keep repeating. Because here's the truth no one likes to admit you can't demand truth from the world if you're not willing to live in it yourself.

The Blame Game Feels Safer, but It's a Trap

I could've easily read his words and said, *"Well, he hurt me more."* But that's the trap, when we measure wounds instead of owning our role.

It's easy to say it's his fault. It's easy to say your boss never gave you a chance. That your friends never supported you. That your parents didn't show up for you.

And some of that may be true. But the danger is when we stop there, when we blame everything external and never turn inward.

Think about work for a moment. That promotion you've been yearning for, it's easy to blame your boss for not recognizing your talent. But what if you paused and asked yourself: *"Have I really shown up at my best? Have I made my contributions visible?"*

Sis, you might be surprised at what you uncover when you move from blame to honest self-reflection.

Check Yourself

If you really want to know how well you're taking accountability, start here:

- Have you ever stayed in a relationship long after you knew it was over, then blamed the man for how miserable you felt?
- Have you ever gotten defensive when a friend gave you feedback you didn't want to hear?
- Have you ever shut down emotionally, yet expected others to keep showing up for you?

Sis, I'm not judging, I've done it too. We all have. The goal isn't to feel shame, it's to get honest. Because honesty is where change begins.

Real Friends Will Check You

Accountability is hard to grow alone. That's why my circle matters so much. They love me, but they don't let me slide.

I don't surround myself with women who just nod and agree with everything I say. I keep friends who will pull me aside and say, *"That didn't make sense, sis."* And I value that because it means I'm surrounded by people who want to see me grow, not just feel good.

I remember once venting about my ex, going on and on about how wrong he was. One of my friends stopped me mid-sentence and said,

"Now Yanique, you know that's not entirely true. At some point, you have to accept your role in this."

Did I like hearing that? Nope. I brushed it off and kept my victim badge polished. But years later, when I read my ex's survey response, her words came back to me. And I had to admit…she was right.

The Victim Trap

Some of us have gotten comfortable being the victim. We've wrapped our identity in what happened to us. We've made our pain our personality. But here's the thing: what happened to you may not be your fault, but how you carry it forward *is* your responsibility.

Being hurt doesn't excuse hurting others. Being tired doesn't justify disrespect. Being abandoned doesn't mean you can abandon accountability.

Take a pause, breathe, and come back to the conversation when your tone matches your intentions. When you stay in victim mode, you delay your own breakthrough. When you own your part, you unlock your next level.

Accountability Doesn't Diminish You, it Grows You

Admitting you were wrong doesn't make you weak, it makes you wise.
It means you're not stuck in your ego.
It means you're prioritizing growth over what people think of you.

It's saying, *"Yes, I could've handled that better, and I plan to do better next time."*
It's choosing to break cycles, not repeat them.
It's realizing that being real with yourself is the most powerful love you can give yourself.

Signs You Might Be Avoiding Accountability

- You always find a way to make someone else the problem.
- You say, "That's just how I am" instead of working on your bad habits.
- You get defensive when people offer feedback, even if it's gentle.
- You refuse to apologize unless someone else apologizes first.
- You replay stories that make you the hero and others the villain.

Sis…if you nodded at any of those, don't beat yourself up. Just recognize it. Awareness is the first step to change.

Grace + Growth Can Coexist

This chapter isn't meant to shame you. This is your nudge to rise higher.

You can forgive yourself and hold yourself accountable.
You can love yourself and still challenge yourself to do better.
You can own your healing without outsourcing your growth.

That's what maturity looks like.
That's what womanhood looks like.
That's what becoming HER looks like.

Sis, one of the most powerful things you'll ever do is say: *"I was wrong, and I'm ready to do better."*

Full Circle

Remember my ex? Reaching out to him wasn't about justifying his actions or excusing mine. It was about owning my truth so I could walk lighter.

And that's the thing, healing opens the door, but accountability hands you the key. Once you take it, there's no limit to what you can walk into.

Sis, accountability doesn't weaken you, it unlocks you. It's the bridge between who you've been and who you're becoming. Healing opens the door, but accountability hands you the key. And once you grab that key, you step into a new level of worthiness. Now it's time to talk about what happens when you stand in that worth: you start attracting what you truly deserve.

HER Mirror Moment: Sis, Say It Out Loud

"I take full ownership of my growth. I am honest with myself. I am open to feedback. I am committed to becoming better, not bitter."

HER Word: Sis, Let's reflect

At the end of the day, you own your growth. No one else can carry that for you. The truth is no one can do that inner work for you. These reflection prompts will help you pause, get real, and take responsibility for the life you're building.

Your Reflection Questions

1. What's one area of your life where you've been blaming others but need to take ownership?

2. Who in your life gives you real, loving accountability? How do you usually respond to it?

3. What would change if you stopped making excuses and just made a decision to grow?

4. How would your relationships, work, or personal goals shift if you consistently owned your part in every situation?

26

SIS, ATTRACT WHAT YOU DESERVE

*"Attraction isn't magic. It's alignment. It's clearing space,
healing wounds, and living today like the woman you want to
become tomorrow."*
— **Yanique P. Walters**

Have you ever heard the saying that the universe is listening and you should be careful what you speak and think? That's because the universe is indeed listening, and Sis, it's time to be intentional about what you put out there.

We attract what we focus on. The more you speak negativity, doubt, or fear, the more your reality begins to mirror those thoughts. Your brain is wired to follow your dominant thoughts, and the universe doesn't recognize sarcasm, it moves in the direction of your energy.

Let me say this loud and clear: **you attract what you believe you deserve.**

If you want peace, you can't keep entertaining chaos. If you want love, you can't stay replaying heartbreak. The first step to attracting the right job, the right man, the right home, or the right energy is to live like you deserve it, not from delusion, but from alignment.

Preparing for What You Want

Let me show you what I mean.

In 2008, I visited the United States for the first time. I was so excited. I landed in Orlando, worked at Universal Studios, that was magical! And for the first time, I got a taste of life in America. I even signed up for my first credit card from Bank of America.

Now, unlike my peers who closed their accounts after returning to Jamaica, I kept mine open. Why? Because I knew America was going to be my home one day. And I knew credit mattered here. Fast-forward to today, I live in the US, and that card became my longest-standing line of credit, opening doors for auto loans and more.

That's what manifestation looks like: preparation meeting vision. I didn't just wish for it; I prepared for it.

And that's the same way we must treat relationships, opportunities, and healing; prepare for their arrival.

Making Room for the New

Steve Harvey once told a story that made this truth so plain. He wanted a new car, but his old one sat in the driveway up on blocks. Every time his mom asked about it, he said, "Soon." One day, she told him, "Son, you'll never get a new car if you don't clear the old one out of the way."

Sure enough, after he finally got rid of it, the new car came.

The same applies to us. You can't hold on to dead weight and expect God to bless you with better. Sis, you can't be texting your ex while asking God to send your husband. Clear the emotional driveway.

Healing Before Attracting

I had to learn this the hard way. After my divorce, I thought I was ready to date again. But whew, epic fail.

I was suspicious, guarded, reactive, and didn't even realize it. Later, I looked back at old text exchanges and was shocked at how aggressive, impatient, and defensive I had been. I wasn't healed. I was hurting. And because of that, I kept attracting from pain instead of from peace.

Therapy helped me see the difference. Today, I know my worth. I know my peace matters. And I know I want to be someone else's peace too. That means: if a man can't add to my peace, he's not my man. I now know how not to be and how to spot when I am being like that in the future because no one deserve that kind of treatment for bruise they didn't inflict.

Choosing Peace Over Bitterness

Healing wasn't just about dating; it was about co-parenting too.

After the divorce, I wanted so badly to hate my ex. The drama was exhausting. But the more I sat with those feelings, the more I realized:

bitterness bound me, not him. He moved on. Meanwhile, I was the one stuck replaying pain.

I had to make a choice: would I co-parent with grace, or would I use my child as a weapon?

Using my child was not an option so I chose peace. I chose cooperation. I chose to let my son grow up loved, not trapped in a war that ended years ago.

Sis, forgiveness is for *your* freedom, not theirs. You don't have to forget. You can forgive and still have boundaries. But don't let bitterness be the baggage you carry into your next season.

Check Your Energy

And it's not just me, the survey proved it too.

When I asked men why they stayed in relationships they no longer cared for, many admitted: "sex," "comfort," or "convenience." But when I asked women why they stayed, most answered: "loneliness," "fear," or "hoping he'd change."

Sis, that right there shows the danger of unhealed attraction. Brokenness attracts brokenness. Healing attracts wholeness.

Here's the real question: **are you who you're praying for?**

If you want a generous man, are you generous yourself? If you want consistency, are you consistent? If you want someone who dreams, are you dreaming too?

You attract what you prepare for.

Stop Shrinking, Start Shining

There was a time when I tried to dim my light to fit in. I talked softer, played smaller, compromised just to belong. I thought maybe I was too bold, too ambitious, too much.

But the truth? I wasn't too much. They were simply not enough.

Stop adjusting your personality to make others comfortable. Adjust your circle to be more supportive. You don't need to become less so someone else can feel like more. Sis, shine anyway.

Because here's the truth: **self-respect is magnetic.** The right people won't run from your standards; they'll respect them. High standards don't repel the right ones; they filter out the wrong ones.

What You Prepare For, You Attract

Sis, you don't just get what you ask for, you get what you prepare for.

That means:

- Asking God in prayer for the things you need.
- Cleaning up your spirit and your space.
- Living with intention and purpose.
- Speaking life over your future.
- Showing up as the woman who's already walking in her blessing, even if it hasn't arrived yet.

Stop settling for attention when you want intention. Likes aren't love. Compliments aren't commitment. Crumbs aren't a feast. Don't mistake temporary attention for lasting devotion.

Sis, you can't keep holding on to what drains you and still expects God to deliver what fulfills you. Release the distractions, clear the space, and remember this: you are still **HER**. And if you've forgotten, the next chapter will remind you exactly how to rise into her.

HER Mirror Moment: Sis, Say It Out Loud

"I am aligned, worthy, and open to receive as much as I want. I no longer chase, *I attract* everything meant for me with ease, peace, and confidence."

HER Word: Sis, Let's Reflect

It's that time again …Grab your *"Her Reflection"* journal and give yourself the space to reflect. These aren't just questions, they're keys to unlocking your next level.

Your Reflection Questions

1. What are you still holding on to that could be blocking your blessings?
2. What kind of partner, job, or opportunity are you praying for, and are you also preparing for it?
3. How can you shift your energy or habits to reflect what you truly want?
4. Does what you want to align with what you're currently tolerating?

SIS, HERE'S THE TRUTHS I HAD TO LEARN

Sis, these are the things I wish I knew that I want you to take away from **PART FIVE**

Chapter 21: Sis, Single Life is not Punishment

- Being single is not a punishment, it's a season of alignment, clarity, and preparation.
- You're not behind in life just because you're not in a relationship.
- Don't let society's deadlines or family pressure push you into settling.
- Healing in your single season keeps you from tolerating placeholders.
- Be intentional, prayerful, and patient when choosing a partner.
- Don't compare your journey to someone else's highlight reel.

Chapter 22: Sis, Be True to Who You Are

- You don't have to become who they want, you just need to remember who you are.
- Your authenticity is your superpower.
- It's okay to outgrow environments where your truth makes people uncomfortable.
- Staying true to yourself might cost you people, but it will never cost you peace.
- The right people won't require you to shrink or pretend.

Chapter 23: Sis, Gratitude is a Must

- Gratitude doesn't mean settling for less, it means seeing beauty even while you grow.
- The more you give thanks, the more you recognize what's *already* working.
- Gratitude shifts your focus from lack to abundance.
- You can be grateful *and* still desire more.
- Sometimes, the smallest blessings are the loudest reminders that you're not alone.

Chapter 24: Sis, Who Are You Without the Pain?

- Pain shaped you, but it's not your identity.
- Healing means choosing to live, not just survive.
- You are not broken, you are layered.
- You don't owe your future self a life built from wounds.
- You're allowed to be someone new—joyful, whole, and free.

Chapter 25: Sis, Take Accountability

- Healing isn't just about what they did, it's about how *you* responded and what you'll do next.
- Accountability is not shame, it's power.
- Growth begins when blame ends.
- You can't change the past, but you can choose not to repeat it.
- Being honest with yourself is the highest form of self-respect.

Chapter 26: Sis, Attract What You Deserve

- You attract what you believe you're worthy of.
- High standards don't make you difficult, they make you intentional.
- You don't have to chase what's aligned with you.
- Self-worth is magnetic.
- If you want something different, you must *be* different.

PART SIX

Rising Into HER (Heal, Evolve and Reclaim What's Yours)

You've shed the weight of who you were. Now it's time to rise as the woman you are becoming

SIS, YOU ARE STILL HER

"Even after the heartbreak, the doubt, and the detour, you're still HER. Healed. Empowered. Resilient."
— **Yanique P. Walters**

Y ou have always been her. If somewhere along the way you forgot, then Sis, it's time to reintroduce yourself. No man, no job, no heartbreak, no baby, no setback can erase who you are at your core. She never left. She's just been waiting, patiently and quietly, for you to come back home to yourself.

Remember the First Time You Loved Yourself

Before the heartbreaks, before the self-doubt, before life tried to harden you — there was a version of you who believed she could have everything. She laughed without holding back. She walked into rooms without shrinking. She dreamed out loud.

That girl wasn't naive — she was whole.

And the truth is, she didn't disappear.
She simply got buried under:

- Expectations
- Survival mode
- Responsibilities
- Disappointment
- And the pressure to be "strong"

This chapter is your invitation to **exhale**, to soften your shoulders, to unclench your jaw, to release the weight you were never meant to carry alone.

This isn't about becoming. It's about remembering. It's about reclaiming. It's about returning to the version of you that existed before the world convinced you she wasn't enough. And if you've made it this far, I hope your light feels a little brighter. But just in case doubt still whispers, let this chapter remind you: You were never broken. You were always Her. **Still Her**. Forever Her.

The journey to returning to her starts with how you see yourself, how deeply you believe you deserve better, how willing you are to show up for yourself, not just in theory, but in practice.

Start With Your Inner Child
I want you to write a letter to your younger self. Yes, that little girl who had big dreams before the world told her who she should be. Apologize

for the things you accepted in the name of love that didn't serve you; for staying when you should've walked away, for shrinking yourself to fit into someone else's small box. Reassure her: "I see you now. I'm choosing you now."

Reclaim Your Routine

Becoming HER means taking care of the woman in the mirror. If you've gained or lost weight and feel disconnected from your body, start showing up with love, not shame. If stress has made your skin break out, invest in your glow-up. Start that skincare routine. Take your vitamins. Walk. Stretch. Drink water like it's holy. Let's go shopping, Sis. Stop dressing for who you used to be. Stop wearing the clothes that no longer align with the woman you are becoming. You deserve to feel good, look good, and radiate confidence, even if no one is watching.

Affirm Who You Are

Your inner dialogue matters. Start affirming yourself. Say it out loud and often: "I am whole. I am healing. I am HER." Grab "my affirmation cards" or flip through the ones included in this book. Keep them on your mirror. Tape them to your fridge. Speak to them over yourself daily, until they're no longer affirmations, but reality.

Level Up With Intention

If there's a job you want, pull up that job description and reverse-engineer your path. What qualifications do you need? What skills are missing? Now's the time to invest in you. The same goes for love. Don't sit around waiting for a man to fix your broken pieces. Start building the life you want, so that when love shows up, it's an addition, not a rescue mission.

Cut Off Distractions

Delete every number that still pulls you backward. You know the ones:

The midnight texters. The "wyd" experts. The ones who breadcrumb you just enough to keep you from moving on. Block them. Unfollow them. Tell them, lovingly, "I no longer require your services." Because Sis, you're no longer accepting expired energy.

Embody Her Now

Stop waiting until you feel ready. Start showing up as her today. Speak to yourself with kindness. Walk with intention. Make choices like the version of you who already has the life she prayed for. Write down your non-negotiables — in your career, your friendships, your relationships, and even within your family. Stick to them, especially when it's hard. Especially when it's lonely. Boundaries are your protection, not punishment.

Define Your Three P's

Get clear about what you need in every area of your life:

- **Personal:** What brings you peace? What nourishes your body and soul?
- **Professional:** What will you no longer tolerate in your work life? What does fulfillment look like to you?
- **Partnership:** What values must your partner hold? How must they communicate? What kind of love do you desire?

Stop Settling Out of Scarcity

I remember accepting the first job that came my way after college because I was scared nothing better would come. It worked out in some ways, but I still wonder what would've happened if I waited just a little longer for something more aligned. Don't let fear trick you into thinking "something" is better than "nothing." Not when it comes to life-altering decisions. Don't marry a man just because he came. Don't stay at a job just because they offered you the position. Don't hold onto friendships just because they're familiar or in close proximity. Scarcity mindset leads to survival. But Sis, you weren't born to just survive. You were born to thrive.

HER Is a Lifestyle

HER is not a mood. Not an outfit. Not a "glow up era."
HER is:

- How you speak to yourself
- How you let others treat you
- How you choose peace
- How you honor your needs
- How you refuse to shrink
- How you love without abandoning yourself

HER is **who you are when no one is watching.**

I want to hear wedding bells. I want to see degrees hanging. I want to see you glowing in your purpose, raising your children in peace, and walking into every room like you belong—because you do. And if you don't believe it yet, keep turning these pages, keep doing the work. Because HER? She's closer than you think. But to fully step into her, you've got to release what's holding you back. Sis, it's time to let go to grow.

You are not returning to an old version of you.
You are returning to a wiser, softer, stronger, more grounded version of you.

The version who knows:

- What she deserves

- What she refuses
- And who she is, no matter who stays or leaves

You are not becoming HER. You are **coming home.**

HER Mirror Moment: Sis, Say It Out Loud

"I am no longer available for anything that doesn't align with the woman I am becoming. I choose me, fully and fearlessly."

HER Word: Sis, Let's Reflect

Sis, grab your *"Her Reflection"* journal, it's that time again. Let's pause and get real with ourselves. Becoming HER means checking in with your heart and holding space for your truth. These prompts are here to guide you deeper, not to judge you, but to gently pull the greatness out of you.

Your Reflection Questions

1. What version of yourself are you still holding on to that no longer serves you?
2. What would it look like to fully show up as the woman you're becoming?
3. Where have you been dimming your light, and what's one thing you can do to turn it back on?
4. When was the last time you truly felt proud of yourself and how can you create more moments like that?

28

SIS, LET GO TO GROW

"Every time I released what wasn't meant for me, I made room for what was. Growth didn't come from holding on, it came from finally letting go."
— *Yanique P. Walters*

No sugar-coating. We're healing, right? Doing the inner work, drinking our water, journaling, lighting our candles, and still texting him back even when we know we shouldn't? Still holding space for people who wouldn't hold the door open for us?

Girl, it's time.

Let's talk about the weight you're carrying that has nothing to do with purpose and everything to do with attachment. Sometimes, we're not loyal, we're just used to the chaos.

SIS, YOU ARE HER

Let's run down the list:

- That man who keeps coming in and out of your life like it's a revolving door. The one who disappears every time you talk about your needs but magically reappears the second you're happy? Let... Him... Go... You're not a pit stop.
- That job that claps for your "dedication" with leftover cupcakes from someone else's birthday but won't promote you, no matter how many times you show up early or stay late? Let it go. You're not a seat filler; you're the whole show.
- That friend who knew you before you found your voice and now doesn't like the sound of it. The one who low-key throws shade but wraps it up in "I'm just being real"? Babes… that's not your tribe. Loyalty shouldn't feel like walking on eggshells.
- That family member you keep "tolerating" because y'all share the same DNA but not respect, not peace, not joy? Yeah… them too. Because blood may make you related, but respect is what keeps the relationship alive.

Even the environment you've outgrown—the neighborhood, the routines, the circles of people still doing the same thing, complaining about the same stuff, year after year... You don't owe your future to your past.

And here's the hardest one for many of us: You've gotta let go of the old you. The version of you who stayed quiet to keep the peace. The version that thought being needed was the same as being loved. The you that shrunk herself to be more "likable," more "humble," more digestible to people who were never meant to sit at your table in the first place.

Sis, that version of you was in survival mode. You're not there anymore.

Let me tell you something from my heart: The day I decided to stop begging people to choose me, love me, see me... was the day I started showing up for myself. And you know what? That version of me was so unfamiliar at first that even I didn't recognize her. She spoke differently. Walked differently. Didn't respond to drama. Didn't pick up every phone call. She had boundaries, baby, and a silk pillowcase.

You've gotta be willing to grieve the old version of you... to grow into the one God is calling you to be.

Growth isn't always pretty. Sometimes it's messy. Sometimes it's crying in the shower while saying, "This is for my healing," like you're starring in a dramatic Netflix series.

But on the other side of that release? Peace. Clarity. Confidence. And Energy you didn't know you had.

You see, when you're holding on to the wrong things, the right things will have no space to find you.

Let go of the "almost" relationship. The "someday" promises. The people who only love the old version of you. Let go of the guilt that's not even yours to carry. Let go of trying to explain your heart to people who don't have the capacity to receive it.

It's not your job to babysit their comfort zone while you're suffocating in yours.

Here's how you'll know you're growing:

- You stop oversharing with people who never really listen.

- You don't feel the need to over-explain your boundaries.
- You find yourself dancing in the kitchen again. Smiling for no reason. Sleeping better.
- You finally feel free.

That's growth, Sis. And that's what happens when you let go.

You don't have to hold grudges to protect yourself. You don't have to be bitter to be healed. You don't have to clap back to prove your worth.

Sometimes, the real flex is silence and peace.

And before you say, "But it's hard…" I know. I've been there. I've cried over people who couldn't even send a "hope you're okay" text. I've bent over backward to keep things together when I should've walked away. I've kept doors open for folks who were slamming them in my face behind my back.

But every time I let go, I made space for something better.

Stop sharing your ideas with people who can't even spell "vision." You know the ones: "That's not gonna work," "Be realistic," "Ain't nobody doing that", and yet you're doing it. Keep your circle full of folks who say, "Ooooh, how can I help?" instead of "Why would you do that?"

You only get one ride on this rollercoaster called life, and if you're stuck on tracks other people laid for you, you're missing the thrill of your own purpose.

You'll know you're growing when you no longer feel the need to apologize for the woman you're becoming.

Now, here's the truth: you can't keep doing the same things and expect new results. That's not manifestation, that's madness. If you want a better relationship with your kids, with your partner, with your friends, and with yourself, then you've got to do better too.

Start by checking in with yourself:

- What role did I play in the situation going left?
- How have I made this relationship harder?
- What energy am I bringing to the room?

Because here's the freeing part: once you own your truth, you get to re-write the story. I've reached out, apologized where needed, and released people who didn't clap when I healed. Now I sleep like a baby. Well, like a baby that doesn't wake up screaming every 2 hours. Peace is different when you know you did your part.

We're not perfect. We won't ever be. But if you can look back and say, "I gave it my best," then you've already won.

Growth requires change. Change requires release. And release? It requires courage.

One thing I'm often praised for is my resilience. But the secret? I don't see pain as permanent. I grew up believing in the power of the "9-day wonder." You know—how everybody's business is a hot topic for 9 days max? Well, I took that and flipped it. I remind myself that no matter how hard something feels right now, I won't still be in it 9 days from now, 9 weeks from now, or 9 months from now, if I choose to move forward.

If Hurricane Melissa taught me anything, it's how quickly life can change. So much was lost. So much was shaken. And yet, it reminded us that our greatest treasures are life, peace, and the people we love. We don't have to wait for storms to release what is no longer serving us. We can choose peace before we're forced to find it.

So now I ask myself: *"Is this adding peace or stealing it?"* If it's not peace, it can't stay.

And Sis, when you finally release what's been holding you back, you don't just free yourself, you give every woman watching you permission to rise too. Let's do this together. Let's conquer the world.

HER Mirror Moment: Sis, Say It Out Loud

"I release what no longer aligns with my peace. I trust that what's ahead is greater than what I'm leaving behind. I make room for healing, love, and wholeness. **I am becoming HER.**"

Grab your *"Her Reflection"* journal. Write a letter to the person, habit, thing, or version of yourself you need to release.

HER ASSIGNMENT: Release Letter Exercise

Start with: "Dear [insert name, role, or version of me], I release you…"

Don't sugarcoat it. Be honest, this is your safe space. Write the hurt, the truth, the hope.

Then end with: **"I choose peace. I choose growth. I choose me."**

29

SIS, LET'S CONQUER THE WORLD (TOGETHER)

"You were never meant to do it all alone. Together, we rise —
stronger, louder, and more unstoppable than ever."
— Yanique P. Walters

S is… take a breath.

Not because you're almost at the end of this book, but because you're stepping into a new level of yourself — a level that requires intention, alignment, and community. A level you cannot and should not walk into alone.

For far too long, women have been told to carry everything by themselves.
To be the backbone.

The nurturer.
The problem-solver.
The emotional sponge.
The mother.
The friend.
The safe space.

And we do it — but not without cost.

Because let's be honest:
Motherhood? Doing everyday life? Healing your past? Carrying emotional weight with no break?
None of that is for the weak.
It will stretch you.
It will humble you.
It will drain you if you don't have people who help refill you.

There are days you look at your child, your responsibilities, your silence, and your exhaustion and think,
"Why am I doing all this alone?"

And you're right to ask.
We were never meant to mother alone.
We were never meant to heal alone.
We were never meant to grow alone.

I miss the days when a village raised a child — when aunties, neighbors, cousins, grandmothers, and community all played a part. When rest wasn't a luxury. When help wasn't something you had to beg for. When motherhood didn't feel like a punishment or an endurance test.

But even if the traditional village looks different now, it doesn't mean your village can't still exist.
It just looks different.
It might be smaller.
It might be scattered.
It might be online.
It might be your chosen family.
But Sis — a village is still possible.

And this chapter is about rebuilding yours.

You Were Not Designed To Carry Everything

Yes, you're strong.
Yes, you know how to survive.
Yes, you can get it done.

But strength isn't supposed to be the only thing holding you together.
Strength needs support.
Strength needs rest.
Strength needs connection.

Let me share a personal truth:

I grew up watching a strong mother.
A woman who held life together with her bare hands, who taught me survival, resilience, independence, and discipline. Her strength shaped me... and also silently taught me that needing help was weakness.

So for years, I carried everything alone — responsibilities, emotions, traumas, heartbreak, dreams, motherhood, burdens, bills, and expectations. I wore strength like armor.

But writing this book changed me.

My Story — How Community Held Me

Sis… this book was not written alone.
This healing was not done alone.
This becoming did not happen alone.

I leaned on my people more than ever before.

My friends — Lord knows I bothered them.
My Facebook family — encouraging me in ways they'll never fully understand. My sister group — praying with me, checking on me, laughing with me. And the women on my podcast — my God! They showed up and showed out. Every story, every reflection, every vulnerability poured life into me.

Many of them shared something that stuck with me:
their "codes."
The signals their sisters know to watch for.
The group chat that becomes a lifeline.
The friend who knows something is wrong just from a text.
The tribe that doesn't wait for explanations — they just show up.

It reminded me that community isn't optional — it's vital.

It's holy.
It's healing.
It's necessary.

This book was shaped, strengthened, and supported by a collective.
These women poured into me, and through me, they poured into you.

And I want you to have that same support system — one that holds you up when you're tired, whispers truth when you doubt yourself, and reminds you who you are when life tries to make you forget.

The Version Of You Who Rises In Community

Conquering the world together isn't about perfection — it's about partnership.

It's the future version of you who:

- Chooses discipline even when she's tired.

- Honors her boundaries without apology.

- Walks away from chaos without guilt.

- Loves herself enough to rest.

- Stops doing motherhood entirely alone

- Builds a circle that pours into her

- Refuses to shrink to make others comfortable

- Trusts her intuition the first time

- Chooses alignment over approval

Believes in her next level even when others can't see it

This chapter is practical because your elevation needs tools, not just motivation.

How To Rise — Practical Steps

Build Your Support Circle Intentionally Identify the people who make you feel safe, grounded, loved, and understood — then nurture those connections.

Create a Consistency Ritual

Commit to one habit for the next 21 days. Consistency builds self-trust.

Release What Drains You

You know exactly who and what I'm talking about.

Strengthen Your Motherhood Village

Whether it's:
- another mom,
- a coworker,
- your sister,
- your best friend,
- an online community...

It counts. Build it. Use it. Lean into it without shame.

Listen to the Future You

Her voice is quiet, but she knows the way.

Dear FUTURE ME:

Sis, Write to Her — The Future You You've come this far and trust me, there's more in you. So, let's make it official. **Go to www.futureme.org** and write a letter to your future self. Set it to be delivered 6 months or a year from now. Tell her what you hope she's healed from, how far she's come, and remind her of the promises you're making today.

- Speak life into her.

- Encourage her when she may forget.

- Remind her: You didn't come this far to stop now.

This isn't just a letter, it's a seed. And when she opens it? She'll see the roots you planted today.

HER Mirror Moment: Sis, Say It Out Loud

"I am powerful. I am worthy. I am ready. The world is mine, and I am walking in my purpose with confidence and grace."

HER Word: Sis, Lets Reflect

Before you close this chapter, take one last moment with yourself. These final questions are a chance to anchor everything you've learned and everything you've become. No pressure, no perfection, just honesty.

Sis, one last time, grab your *"Her Reflection"* journal.

Your Reflection Questions

1. What's one thing you are committed to doing for yourself from this day forward?

2. How will you show up for yourself like never before?

3. What legacy do you want to leave for the next generation of women?

4. Who do you need to become in order to conquer the world in your own unique way?

Sis, Here's the Truth I Had to Learn

These are the things I wish I knew early that I want you to take away from **PART SIX**

Chapter 27: Sis, You Are Still HER

- Even after the heartbreak, mistakes, and detours, you are still HER.
- Your power didn't disappear; it's just been waiting for your permission to rise.
- Healing doesn't make you less, it makes you unstoppable.
- You don't need to prove anything. You just need to *remember who you are.*
- The crown never left, you just forgot how to wear it.

Chapter 28: Sis, Let go to Grow

- Sometimes we're not loyal, we're just used to the chaos.
- You're not a pit stop; you're the destination. Stop letting people treat you like a revolving door.
- Blood makes you related, but respect keeps you connected.
- The old you were in survival mode. The new you are in healing mode.
- The day I stopped begging people to choose me was the day I chose myself.
- You don't have to clap back to prove your worth. Sometimes the real flex is silence and peace.
- If it doesn't add peace, it has to go.
- Growth requires release. Release requires courage.

Chapter 29: Sis, Let's Conquer the World (Together)

- You were never meant to do this alone. Community is part of your healing.
- Empowered women *empower* women.
- Collaboration over competition always wins.
- Your success doesn't threaten mine; it expands the vision for all of us.
- When we rise together, we change the world.

REFLECTION

Sis, Pause and Look Back

This isn't just about what you've learned. It's about who you've become. Let's honor that before you pass the torch.

30

SIS, LOOK HOW FAR YOU'VE COME

"You may not be where you want to be yet, but Sis, take a breath, take a bow. You're not who you used to be either."
— *Yanique P. Walters*

S is, you made it to the end! If you're reading this, it means you didn't give up. You stayed. You leaned in. You cried, reflected, maybe even laughed, but most of all, you showed up for YOU.

So go ahead: pat yourself on the back, give yourself a big hug, and scream in the mirror, **"I did it. I did the work."**

I hope you feel that. I hope something shifted. I hope your eyes are more open, your spirit more grounded, and that you're stepping into the world as a more whole, more confident version of you.

And more than anything, I hope you finally realize... **She was in there all along.** You just had to wake up the lioness inside of you.

You are amazing. And I'm so proud that you chose to walk this journey with me.

Writing this book changed me too. The research, the conversations, the reflection, all revealed things I didn't even realize I was still working through. I told y'all from the start, I'm not perfect. And this process reminded me of that. But I'm grateful, because I got to compile this report, this truth, this gift — just for you. To help you walk away stronger, more empowered, and more aligned.

Sis, there are going to be naysayers, those who will not understand your new journey. If it means walking alone, you must choose to do that, because looking back is not the answer. Keep going.

You are not the same woman who opened this book. Even if your life hasn't changed yet, you have. Your thoughts are shifting. Your standards are rising. Your peace is now a priority.

This book isn't the finish line; it is the beginning.

So, whether you're still healing, setting boundaries, dating with discernment, or finally choosing yourself, you've got what it takes to keep becoming her.

Keep doing the work.
Keep shining.
Keep glowing.
Because Sis... **you are just getting started.**

A Prayer for You

Dear God,
I'm praying for the woman reading this right now. She's taken the time to invest in herself. She's shown that she wants better; for her mind, her heart, and her life.
I pray peace over her life.
I pray that real love finds her, first from within, and then from others.
I pray her confidence returns stronger than ever. That she starts to see her worth clearly and never questions it again.
May she no longer ignore red flags or stay where she isn't cherished.
May she boldly recognize when someone is intentional, and when they are not.
Lord, I place her in your hands.
Cover her, guide her, and continue to nurture her growth.
Amen.

HER Word: Sis, Let's Reflect

Take a few minutes. Grab your *"Her Reflection"* journal. Be still. Be honest. You've come so far, so honor that growth. Answer these in your journal:

Your Reflection Questions

1. What surprised you the most about your own growth?

2. What are three things you are proud of yourself for?

3. What truth will you carry with you from this journey?

4. What changes will you be making?

31

SIS, PASS THE TORCH

"The healed version of you is someone else's blueprint. Don't just rise. Reach back, and light the way."
— Yanique P. Walters

The journey doesn't stop with you, it expands because of you. You've done the inner work. You've faced the mirror. You've spoken the truth out loud. And now, Sis... it's time to pass the torch.

Somewhere out there is a younger you: a sister, a friend, a daughter, a coworker, still wrestling with her worth, still questioning if she's enough. Be her light.

Passing the torch doesn't mean you're perfect. It means you're willing. Willing to show up as you are and share what you've learned. Willing to let go of the past and move forward. William to trust and believe in your ability. And willing to say, "it's my turn now."

Your voice matters. Your growth matters. Your testimony is someone else's roadmap.

Here's what I'm asking: Don't gate-keep healing. Don't hide your breakthroughs. Don't shrink when it's your turn to speak up. The same way you once needed someone to show you the way... now you get to be that someone.

- Be the friend who checks in.
- Be the sister who says, "I've been there too."
- Be the mentor who reminds her, "You're not crazy. You're waking up."

You didn't go through all of this just to keep it to yourself. You are a torchbearer now. Keep the flame alive. Light the way. And let's keep building this movement, one healed woman at a time.

Sis, this is what I've learned...

- You are not your trauma response.
- You are not your survival story.
- You are not defined by how much pain you can carry.
- You are allowed to *be*, without explaining, fixing, or proving.

Your identity is not just what you've overcome, it's who you are when you're safe, rested, and free.

Join the Movement

Now it's time to keep going. To keep reinforcing everything you've learned. Because this isn't the end, it's your launch.

So, Sis... grab the tools that will walk this next season with you:

- Grab the "**Her Reflection**" Journal to help you reflect on this journey.
- Grab the "**Her Mirror**" affirmation cards" to keep your mindset strong.
- Grab the "*Her* **Healing**" game to challenge and empower your growth in the community.
- Grab the "*Her* **Boundary**" cards to help you stand firm in your worth.
- Grab the "*Her* **Gaslighting**" cards to remind you of what's real, and what's manipulation.

You've done the work. Now it's time to keep the momentum.

You are **HER**. You always were. And now, the world gets to see it too.

Follow us on Instagram @sisyouareher.

Join our Facebook group - Sis, You Are HER

ACKNOWLEDGMENTS

With Gratitude

Thank you for taking the time to read this book. I poured my heart into writing, designing, and compiling it in a way that would speak to you, uplift you, and hopefully help you heal. I pray it was beneficial.

To the men and women who completed my survey, thank you. Your insights were honest, vulnerable, and incredibly valuable. Men, I hope you didn't think that this book was written against you. So let me be clear — it was written for her, but with you in mind. You reminded me that not all men are afraid of accountability. That not all men are silent when it comes to healing. That some of you *want* to do better, be better, and support better.

To those who engaged in discussions with me, through shared stories, thoughtful insights, or even heated debates, thank you. I've learned so much about the complex dynamics between men and women, and your voices helped shape the heart of this book.

To my friends Renee Watson, Jodi Johnson, Joshua Robb, and Latoya Berry, thank you for lending your time, your ears, and your opinions. From helping me choose the title to weighing in on the design and content, your input meant the world to me.

To my sister, Sheena-Gaye, thank you for listening to one of my chapters and then immediately telling me not to read you anymore because you wanted to experience the full book for yourself. Thank you for sharing your insights on design and content. Your excitement and support reminded me why I wrote this in the first place.

To my exes, thank you for the lessons. I'm a firm believer that there's no such thing as a failed relationship. Not everyone is meant to be "the one." Some are simply sent to teach you. And because of those lessons, this book was born.

To my son, Kyng, you are my greatest why. Thank you for allowing me time to write when you wanted nothing more but for me to be laying on the sofa, watching TV with you. Your presence in my life has made me braver, softer, and stronger. Everything I do is to be a better version of myself, for you and because of you.

To God, thank You; for giving me the strength to write this, the wisdom to live through it, and the courage to share it. None of this would have been possible without Your grace and timing.

To everyone who read my book before its release and offered your feedback, I appreciate you deeply. Thank you for seeing my vision, believing in this message, and reminding me how real this book is and how many women will be impacted by it.

To everyone who shared their feedback on my book cover, thank you. Your input, your honesty, and your eye for detail helped shape the beautiful cover you now see. I truly appreciate every comment, every suggestion, and every moment you took to help me bring this vision to life.

To Lamont Sledge — thank you for stepping in with design support right when I needed it. Your willingness to help, your time, and your expertise made a huge difference. I appreciate you more than you know.

To everyone who donated through my Buy Me a Coffee link... whew, thank you! You knew I needed all the caffeine I could get during this process. Your generosity helped bring each part of this project to life

— whether it was software, marketing needs, or printing costs. You played a part in every page, every detail, and every product created.

And to you, the reader, thank you for being here. Thank you for choosing healing. Thank you for choosing you. I hope this book reminded you that you are powerful, precious, and absolutely still **HER**.

Please share your feedback and let me know which chapter resonated with you the most.

I love you all!
Yanique P. Walters

Open When You Forget Who You Are.

Hey Sis,
If you're opening this, it means life got heavy or loud, and maybe you don't feel like *you* right now. That's okay. It happens to the strongest of us. But hear me when I say this:

You are not the pain.
You are not the mistake.
You are the comeback.
You are the woman who keeps rising.

So take a deep breath. Let's remember who you are.

Sis, you've walked through fires that should've taken you out, yet here you are—still choosing truth, still choosing growth. You've survived heartbreak, carried burdens you never asked for, and still, you show up. Maybe quietly, maybe shakily, but you show up.

Forgetting who you are doesn't make you weak. It makes you human. Life will test your memory of your own strength. People may mishandle your heart. Seasons may stretch you thin. But none of that changes this truth:

So if you've forgotten who you are, let me remind you:

You are chosen.
You are protected.
You are favored.
You are HER.

Don't count yourself out.

I love you.
Now go remember you.

Companion Journal And Affirmation Cards

Ready to go deeper?

Grab you're **HER Reflection companion journal** or **HER Mirror Affirmation** card deck to fully engage with the prompts in this book. Whether you're writing your truth, setting intentions, or pulling a card for daily reflection—this companion is designed to help you heal, evolve, and reclaim your power in real time.

- **Write it out.**
- **Speak it into being**
- **Reflect honestly.**
- **Grow intentionally.**

Don't just read the words—live them.
Grab your copy and do the work that transforms. You are HER and it's time to start acting like it!

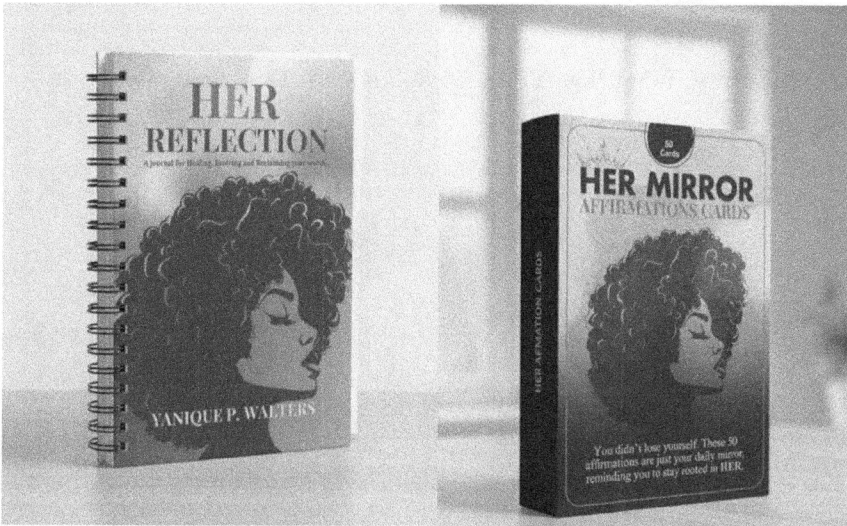

Other Books And Publications

Shop All Books Here - www.yaniquepwalters.com

Gratitude is a Must - Men and Women journal

Younique - Perfectly Imperfect	Womentality
	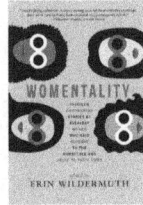

Dear Mommy, What Was Your Life Like	What's Up Dad, Tell me about Your Life.
	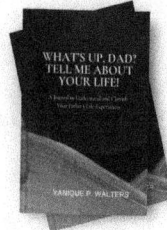

THANK YOU FOR READING!

SCAN TO SHOP & CONNECT